RESILIENT

RESILIENT

Restoring Your Weary Soul in These Turbulent Times

JOHN ELDREDGE

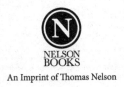

NELSON
BOOKS

An Imprint of Thomas Nelson

Resilient

© 2022 by John Eldredge

All rights reserved. No portion of this book may be reproduced, stored in a retrieval system, or transmitted in any form or by any means—electronic, mechanical, photocopy, recording, scanning, or other—except for brief quotations in critical reviews or articles, without the prior written permission of the publisher.

Published in Nashville, Tennessee, by Nelson Books, an imprint of Thomas Nelson. Nelson Books and Thomas Nelson are registered trademarks of HarperCollins Christian Publishing, Inc.

Published in association with Yates & Yates, www.yates2.com.

Thomas Nelson titles may be purchased in bulk for educational, business, fundraising, or sales promotional use. For information, please email SpecialMarkets@ThomasNelson.com.

Any internet addresses, phone numbers, or company or product information printed in this book are offered as a resource and are not intended in any way to be or to imply an endorsement by Thomas Nelson, nor does Thomas Nelson vouch for the existence, content, or services of these sites, phone numbers, companies, or products beyond the life of this book.

Unless otherwise noted, Scripture quotations are taken from the Holy Bible, New International Version®, NIV®. Copyright © 1973, 1978, 1984, 2011 by Biblica, Inc.® Used by permission of Zondervan. All rights reserved worldwide. www.zondervan.com. The "NIV" and "New International Version" are trademarks registered in the United States Patent and Trademark Office by Biblica, Inc.® Scripture quotations marked AMP are taken from the Amplified® Bible (AMP). Copyright © 2015 by The Lockman Foundation. Used by permission. www.Lockman.org. Scripture quotations marked ESV are taken from the ESV® Bible (The Holy Bible, English Standard Version®). Copyright © 2001 by Crossway, a publishing ministry of Good News Publishers. Used by permission. All rights reserved. Scripture quotations marked THE MESSAGE are taken from THE MESSAGE. Copyright © 1993, 2002, 2018 by Eugene H. Peterson. Used by permission of NavPress. All rights reserved. Represented by Tyndale House Publishers, a Division of Tyndale House Ministries. Scripture quotations marked NASB are taken from the New American Standard Bible® (NASB). Copyright © 1960, 1962, 1963, 1968, 1971, 1972, 1973, 1975, 1977, 1995, 2020 by The Lockman Foundation. Used by permission. www. Lockman.org. Scripture quotations marked NASB1995 are taken from the New American Standard Bible® (NASB). Copyright © 1960, 1962, 1963, 1968, 1971, 1972, 1973, 1975, 1977, 1995 by The Lockman Foundation. Used by permission. www.Lockman.org. Scripture quotations marked NET are taken from the NET Bible® copyright ©1996–2017 by Biblical Studies Press, L.L.C. http://netbible. com. All rights reserved. Scripture quotations marked NKJV are taken from the New King James Version®. Copyright © 1982 by Thomas Nelson. Used by permission. All rights reserved. Scripture quotations marked NLT are taken from the Holy Bible, New Living Translation. Copyright © 1996, 2004, 2015 by Tyndale House Foundation. Used by permission of Tyndale House Ministries, Carol Stream, Illinois 60188. All rights reserved. Scripture quotations marked NLV are taken from the New Life Version. © 1969, 2003 by Barbour Publishing, Inc. Scripture quotations marked NRSV are taken from New Revised Standard Version Bible. Copyright © 1989 National Council of the Churches of Christ in the United States of America. Used by permission. All rights reserved worldwide. Scripture quotations marked YLT are taken from Young's Literal Translation. Public domain.

ISBN 978-1-4002-0864-7 (HC)
ISBN 978-1-4002-0868-5 (eBook)
ISBN 978-1-4002-3782-1 (ITPE)

Library of Congress Control Number: 2022932089

Printed in the United States of America
22 23 24 25 26 LSC 10 9 8 7 6 5 4 3 2

To Sam and Susie, Blaine and Em, Luke and Liv:
Time with you makes me a more resilient man!

He has made his people strong.
PSALM 148:14 NLT

Contents

No Ordinary Moment

C amels have an Achilles' heel; this is where we will begin.

But their vulnerability is hidden by their legendary *resilience*: these famous "ships of the desert" have been crossing dune seas since before the time of Abraham.

The stamina and strength of camels is truly impressive— they can carry heavy loads across leagues of burning desert sand, going without water for weeks while their human companions die of thirst. But the treacherous thing about camels is that they will walk a thousand miles with seemingly endless endurance, giving you little indication they are about to collapse. Then it just happens. As the Alchemist said to Santiago,

> Camels are traitorous: they walk thousands of paces and never seem to tire. Then suddenly, they kneel and die. But horses tire bit by bit. You always know how much

you can ask of them, and when it is that they are about to die.[1]

Human souls hide an Achilles' heel too.

We have an astonishing capacity to rally in the face of calamity and duress. We rally and rally, and then one day we discover there's nothing left. Our soul simply says, *I'm done; I don't want to do this anymore*, as we collapse into discouragement, depression, or just blankness of soul.

You don't want to push your soul to that point.

But *everything* about the hour we are living in is pushing our souls to that very point. Some folks are nearly there.

We entered the COVID-19 pandemic of 2020 worn out by the madness of modern life. Now, this isn't a book about the pandemic, though when history tells our story COVID-19 will be our generation's World War II—the global catastrophe we lived through. What began in 2020 was a shared experience of global trauma, and trauma takes a toll—the long experience of losses great and small, all the high-volume tension around masks, quarantines, vaccines, school closures, and on and on the list goes. Journalist Ed Yong won the 2021 Pulitzer Prize for Explanatory Reporting for his coverage of the pandemic. Here's what he found:

> Millions have endured a year of grief, anxiety, isolation, and rolling trauma. Some will recover uneventfully, but for others, the quiet moments after adrenaline fades and normalcy resumes may be unexpectedly punishing. When they finally get a chance to exhale, their breaths

may emerge as sighs. "People put their heads down and do what they have to do, but suddenly, when there's an opening, all these feelings come up," Laura van Dernoot Lipsky, the founder and director of the Trauma Stewardship Institute, told me. . . . "As hard as the initial trauma is," she said, "it's the aftermath that destroys people."[2]

Right now we're in a sort of global denial about the actual cost of these hard years (which are not over). We just want to get past it all, so we're currently trying to comfort ourselves with some sense of recovery and relief. But folks, we haven't yet paid the psychological bill for all we've been through. We would never tell a survivor of abuse that the trauma must be over now that the abuse has stopped. And yet that mentality is at play in our collective denial of the trauma we've been through.

We need to be kinder to our souls than that. Denial heals nothing, which is why I'm more concerned about what's coming than what lies behind. In our compromised condition we're now facing some of the trials Jesus warned us about as we approach what the Scriptures refer to as "the end of the age" (Matthew 24:3).

Extraordinary times can be thrilling, but they also tend to be very demanding. Our hearts will need guidance and preparation. It would be a good idea to take the strength of your soul seriously at this time.

In case you've already forgotten what the pandemic was like, allow me to refresh your memory. Fear of death suddenly swept the world, death unseen and unpredictable, death by plague. In a matter of weeks, we found ourselves in various forms of quarantine and lockdown—schools, churches, and businesses all closed their doors. The economy reeled. Everything that makes for a joyful, normal life was taken from us in a moment and withheld for many, many months.

Follow me closely now. To be suddenly stripped of your normal life; to live under the fear of suffering and death; to be bombarded with negative news, kept in a state of constant uncertainty about the future, with no clear view of the finish line; and to lose every human countenance behind a mask—may I point out that this is exactly the torment that terrorist regimes use to break down prisoners psychologically and physically?

Folks, this had a traumatic effect, and we've got to plan for our recovery and find new resilience.

"At least we can get back to our normal lives," one friend said. But that's not true either. I know you *want* it to be true, but events are converging that prevent normal life from happening. Our enemy, the prince of darkness, has engineered this situation to do serious harm to the human heart. I believe we are set up for a sweeping loss of faith.

There is hope, great hope. Jesus Christ knew that humanity would face hard times, especially as history accelerates toward the end of the age. He gave us counsel on how to live through such trials, and now would be a good time to pay attention to what he said. The Creator and Redeemer of our humanity has given us a path toward recovery and resilience. We would be fools to ignore it or push it off to "some other time." Whatever you believe about the coming years, I think we can all agree that greater resilience of heart and soul would be a very good thing to take hold of.

In this hour we don't need inspiration and cute stories. We need a survival guide—which is exactly what this book is. Each chapter opens with a true story of human resilience against the bleakest odds. You'll also encounter "Skills" callouts to draw your attention to practical tools for strengthening heart and soul. And every chapter will pull your attention to Jesus himself, for we need the supernatural resilience provided in Christ. It is always available—we simply have to take hold of it.

LIVING WATER

___

In 1946 Wilfred Thesiger made an impossible trek across the desolate Empty Quarter of Arabia with four Bedouins, journeying in winter on camelback. They reached a desperate point in their odyssey when the odds looked grim—they were nearly out of water, the next well was beyond an impassable mountain range of dunes, and their camels were showing signs of collapsing.

> *All the skins were sweating and we were worried about our water. There had been a regular and ominous drip from them throughout the day, a drop falling to the sand as we rode along, like blood dripping from a wound that could not be staunched. . . .*
>
> *I suppose I was weak from hunger, for the food which we ate was a starvation ration, even by Bedouin standards. But my thirst troubled me most. . . . I was always conscious of it. Even when I was asleep I dreamt of racing streams of ice-cold water, but it was difficult to get to sleep. . . .*
>
> *I worried about the water which I had watched dripping away on to the sand, and about the state of our camels.[1]*

The survivor's first need is water. You can live forty days without food, but only three without water. Water is life; finding water is one of your first objectives.

Chapter 1

I Just Want Life to Be Good Again

Restore the sparkle to my eyes.
PSALM 13:3 NLT

The longing for things to be good again is one of the deepest yearnings of the human heart. It has slumbered in the depths of our souls ever since we lost our true home. For our hearts remember Eden.

Most of the time this beautiful, powerful longing flows like an underground river below the surface of our awareness—so long as we are consoled by some measure of goodness in our lives. While we are enjoying our work, our family, our adventures, or the little pleasures of this world, the longing for things to be good again seems to be placated.

But when trials and heartbreaks wash in, the longing

rises to the surface like a whale coming up for air, filled with momentum and force. This is especially true after times of severe testing, because during the testing we are rallying. But when the storm subsides, the longing for things to be good again rises up to demand relief.

How we shepherd this longing—so crucial to our identity and the true life of our heart—how we listen to it but also guide it in right or wrong directions, this determines our fate.

The Drive That Propels Us

God has given each human soul a capacity and drive, a primal aspiration for life. This is as fundamental to you as your own survival.

The epicenter of our being is the deep longing to *aspire* for things that bring us life, to *plan* for those things, to *take hold* of them, to *enjoy* them, and start the cycle over as we aspire toward new things! This is the essential craving for life given to us by God. Let's call this capacity the Primal Drive for Life.

The longing for things to be good again is the mournful cry of the Primal Drive for Life in us, like the haunting cries of whales under the sea.

> It seems to me we can never give up longing and wishing while we are thoroughly alive. There are certain things we feel to be beautiful and good, and we must hunger after them.[2]

This hunger allows human beings to survive the most terrible ordeals; it also enables us to savor all the goodness of this world, to love, and to create works of immense beauty.

I've long enjoyed Saint John of the Cross's poetry about the soul's intimacy with God. So I was shocked and appalled to discover that this dear man was, at one point in his life, unjustly imprisoned and tortured.

In 1577, as a result of the attempted reform of the Carmelite order and his alliance with St. Teresa [of Avila], he was kidnapped and imprisoned at Toledo. It was during this period of debased confinement and torture . . . that he miraculously composed some of his greatest poetry.

For much of the nine months St. John was in prison, he was confined to a tiny cell, actually an unlit closet in which he could not even stand up. He was left to relieve himself on the floor of this tiny cell, and his few scraps of food and water were sometimes thrown into his feces and urine. On a regular basis he was brought from his cell and beaten . . . to the extent that he became permanently crippled. He was not given a change of clothes or allowed to wash for months. He became infested with lice and dysentery. He was forced to sleep upon his own excrement.[3]

Saint John prevailed and brought enormous beauty to the world from his ordeals. His Primal Drive for Life was imbued by God with a supernatural resilience.

So Very Thirsty

Our Primal Drive for Life has taken a real beating over the past few years.

It isn't only the pandemic. We were all running like rats on a wheel *before* 2020—addicted to technology, overwhelmed by global news, wrung out from social tensions, exhausted body and soul from the madness of modern life. Does anybody even remember? Life was *draining*. It wasn't like we stepped out of a three-year sabbatical when we stepped into 2020. We were set up to be steamrolled by the pandemic.

Then came the repeated cycles of fear, control, chronic disappointment, all those losses great and small, the inability to make plans for the future. This throttled our capacity for living, just as serial rejection harms our ability for relationship, or chronic failure cripples our capacity for hope. We started reaching for relief.

Stasi and I were among the sixty-two *million* homeowners who did renovations during the pandemic—that's more than three-quarters of all homeowners in the US, the highest levels ever seen.[4] We painted the living room, got new carpet, new chairs. We upgraded our garden as well. This was far more than boredom or the desire for change; it was a profound longing for a fresh start *at life* in the midst of so much loss and uncertainty. The renovation craze reflected something deeper—a yearning for life to be good again, expressed in paint and carpet, gardens and landscaping.

But the whole time Stasi and I were renovating our

home, I could feel something was off. The preoccupation of making our home nicer took my mind off the death count in New York, London, Paris, and Delhi, the vicious acrimony over vaccines. But it didn't feel like the answer. It was good; I enjoyed it. But it didn't bring about the fix I was longing for.

Speaking of fixing things, I noticed through the first half of 2021 that I was doing all sorts of obsessive fixing. Everything from a dripping faucet to a lamp that had been wobbly for years—they each seized my attention, and I had to set it right. My soul was desperate to set things right. Haven't you felt this too?

Then life began to return to some semblance of normal—we got restaurants back, movies, outdoor concerts. The world rushed out like the starving survivor of a shipwreck brought back from isolation and set before a Sunday brunch. In the summer of 2021 you couldn't get a rental car, Airbnb, or campsite. Airports, beaches, and national parks were jammed. It was like spring break in Miami. The longing for things to be good again was (and is) raging.

Personally, I couldn't get enough. But all those comforts and activities weren't delivering whatever my soul was desperately longing for.

That Won't Work

One of the most remarkable things about human beings is how resilient we can be. The Primal Drive for Life can accomplish impressive things. Saint John took his suffering and brought forth beauty; Nelson Mandela survived twenty-seven years of imprisonment and brought forth forgiveness.

Yet one of the most surprising things about human beings is how all that resilience can evaporate in a moment.

One day the resources we have to sustain the Primal Drive for Life simply run out. The mother who for decades pours and pours into her family, and then one day up and has an affair with her best friend's husband. The minister who for decades served up banquets from the Word of God suddenly decides he doesn't believe in Jesus anymore.

It has to do with *reserves*.

We tap into our deep reserves to endure years of suffering and deprivation. Then one day our heart simply says, *I don't care anymore; I'm done.* We abandon the fight and go off to find relief. I fear this is what's happening now on a global scale.

Human beings are at the same time both resilient and unpredictably fragile, like camels. A better test for how vulnerable we may *actually* be is to check on our reserves. For we can rally, and we have rallied. Way to go, everybody! But every time you rally, you tap into your reserves, and though you might feel like you're doing pretty well on any given day, you're still burning through precious resources and your reserve tank is precariously low . . . like the drip, drip, dripping water bags of Wilfred Thesiger's party, way out in the middle of the desert.

This is the trauma cycle. We rally in the face of harm, and when the harm subsides, we live in denial of it and go off in search of some taste of Eden. When our efforts

———

One of the most remarkable things about human beings is how resilient we can be. Yet one of the most surprising things about human beings is how all that resilience can evaporate in a moment.

———

are thwarted, rage surfaces—which is common to trauma responses.[5]

This is why rallying can actually be deceptive. Reserves tell the true story.

During the early stages of the pandemic, I circled up my little staff of eighteen wonderful saints (all working online) to check on their well-being. I asked them questions about resilience: "How is your operating strength these days? If you are normally functioning at 100 percent, what are you functioning at now?" Their answers hovered around 30 percent. Most days they were feeling about 30 percent of their normal strength. This is what trauma does.

"Now tell me about your reserves—if a major crisis were to hit tomorrow, what sort of reserves do you have available?" Their answers averaged about 15 percent—and this is a very resilient group of people!

I asked them the same questions a year later, in 2021. Though things had somewhat improved, they were not reporting soaring scores. How about your own reserves? Have you even assessed them? Allow me to ask you a couple of questions:

- If another pandemic were to sweep across the globe next week, some brand-new deadly threat, and we found ourselves back to quarantines, living under the vague threat of suffering and death, in a state of constant uncertainty about the future, with no clear view of the finish line—how would your heart respond to that?
- Or try this on: Your house or apartment is going to burn down tomorrow, and though everyone will

survive, you will lose everything else. All your belongings, records, valuable documents, precious family keepsakes. You will need to rebuild your entire life. Do you have 100 percent vim and verve for that scenario?

Like I said—we have not yet paid the psychological bill for the COVID-19 pandemic. We tapped deep into our reserves to rally, and we are in no condition to face more trauma . . . let alone the assaults of our enemy. Trauma sensitizes you to more trauma and brings to the surface *past* trauma. You don't get used to it; each new crisis simply piles on the stress.[6]

The treacherous thing about human nature is that the Primal Drive for Life is so compelling we will sacrifice almost anything for it—health, marriages, careers, even our faith. After a time of global trauma and deprivation, the longing rages so we wander off in search of life. But reckless wandering without a clear plan or destination often adds to our suffering rather than bringing relief.

When John Wesley Powell made the first descent of the uncharted Colorado River through the Grand Canyon in 1869, he and his colleagues had no idea of the test that was in store. Wild rapids, unexpected falls, swirling pools that threatened to devour their wooden boats. After weeks of this, several of the crew mutinied. Against all warnings they left the river and tried to find an exit out of the canyon through Apache lands.

Those men were never heard from again.[7]

I fear we are being lured into similar dangers as we grasp for relief from all we have endured.

Return to Me

The exodus of the people of Israel and their journey through the Sinai desert is one of the greatest survival stories of all time. More than two *million* people wandering through a land of sand and barren rock, homeless, looking for the land of abundance, a place to call home. When will life be good again?[8]

There were no real sources of food in that desert. Water was about as scarce as it is on the surface of the moon. A "barren wilderness—a land of deserts and pits, a land of drought and death, where no one lives or even travels" (Jeremiah 2:6 NLT).

This is more than a moment in Jewish history. It is recorded for us as one of the great analogies of human experience, our journey from bondage to freedom, from barrenness to the promised land. Ultimately, it is the precursor to our journey of salvation, from the kingdom of darkness to the kingdom of God.

It is a story about the Primal Drive for Life—where will we take our thirst?

This is *the* choice, *the* test. Always has been, always will be.

This Primal Drive for Life was so compelling it caused thousands of those rescued slaves to mount a rebellion to go back to bondage in Egypt just to have their familiar ways back. Sobering.

> "The heavens are shocked at such a thing and shrink back
> in horror and dismay," says the LORD. "For my people

have done two evil things: They have abandoned me—the fountain of living water. And they have dug for themselves cracked cisterns that can hold no water at all!"

JEREMIAH 2:12–13 NLT

The great alarm the Scriptures are sounding is that our longing for life to be good again will be *the* battleground for our heart. How you shepherd this precious longing, and *if* you shepherd it at all, will determine your fate in this life and in the life to come.

This is playing out in a "postpandemic" world: we only sort of want God; what we *really* want is for life to be good again. If God seems to be helping, awesome. We believe! If he doesn't . . . well, we'll get back to him later, after we chase whatever we think will fill our famished craving.

The first stage of the coming storm is this: we've all run off to find life and joy following years of stress, trauma, and deprivation. But it isn't working; *it won't ever work.* We return to our normal Monday through Friday disappointed, and disappointment will become disillusionment. And disillusionment makes us extremely vulnerable to our enemy.

We must lovingly shepherd our famished thirst back to the source of life.

The River of Life

My longtime friend and publisher Brian Hampton used to tell me, "Put the cookies on the bottom shelf." By which he

---

Our longing for life to be good

again will be *the* battleground

for our heart. How you

shepherd this precious longing,

and *if* you shepherd it at all,

will determine your fate in this

life and in the life to come.

---

meant, "Don't make folks wait until the end of the book to get the help you are offering." Fair enough. Let me give you something right now that will prove enormously helpful. Your appreciation for it will grow as we go on, I promise.

When the human heart and soul experience month after month of disappointment and loss, death rolls in. Dr. Richard Gunderman described the progressive onset of disillusionment as the accumulation of hundreds or thousands of tiny disappointments, each one hardly noticeable on its own.[9] The loss of hope and dreams suffocates the Primal Drive for Life.

But our God has provision for us!

I know, I know—most of you think that what you need right now is three months at the coast. Walking on the beach, drinks on the deck, and with all my heart I hope you find that. But for most of us, a sabbatical in some gorgeous refuge is not available. What *is* available is the River of Life, God himself, in ways we have not yet tapped into.

God wants to make his life available to you. Remember— he's the creator of those beautiful places you wish you could go to for a sabbatical. All that beauty and resilience, all that life comes from God, and he wants to impart a greater measure of himself to you! The life of God is described in Scripture as a river—a powerful, gorgeous, unceasing, ever-renewing, ever-flowing river.

Ezekiel was given a number of beautiful visions, glimpses into the kingdom of God that permeates this world. He saw the temple of God in Jerusalem, and out of the temple was flowing the River of Life. As it flowed forth across the countryside, it became so deep and wide it wasn't possible to swim across it—an image of abundance! I love how the passage ends: "Where the river flows everything will live" (Ezekiel 47:9).

Everything will live. This is what we want—to live, to find life in its fullness again.

The apostle John was given a revelation of the coming kingdom and the restored earth, and he saw the River of Life flowing right down the middle of the city of God:

> Then the angel showed me the river of the water of life, as clear as crystal, flowing from the throne of God and of the Lamb down the middle of the great street of the city. On each side of the river stood the tree of life, bearing twelve crops of fruit, yielding its fruit every month. And the leaves of the tree are for the healing of the nations. (Revelation 22:1–2)

There is so much life flowing from God that it flows like a mighty river. Isn't that marvelous? Follow me now—the River of Life is not just for later. Jesus stated clearly that the river is meant to flow out of our inner being right here, in *this* life: "Let anyone who is thirsty come to me and drink. Whoever believes in me, as Scripture has said, rivers of living water will flow from within them" (John 7:37–38).

The mighty life of God flowing in you and through you, saturating you like a river.

Now let me pull all this together. We have a capacity and drive in us for living. It's a precious longing, and it's taken a beating. God is "the fountain of life" (Psalm 36:9). There is so much life flowing from God that it flows like a river no one can even swim across—a superabundant out-flow of life! This life is meant to flow *in* us, and *through* us.

Skill
RECEIVING THE RIVER OF LIFE

_____

In order to tap into the River of Life, we begin by loving God in our longing for life to be good again. That's where things are decided. Nearly all of us have been chasing relief in a myriad of hopes, plans, and dreams without first turning to God. So we need to enter the longing, feel it, become present to it, and in that place start loving God. Choose him.

Our first step toward resilience is to return our Primal Drive for Life and our longing for things to be good again to God; we come back to Jesus from all other places we've been chasing life. We allow him to be our rescuer here, in the longing for life to be good again. We ask God to fill us with the river of his life.

> *Jesus, I come back to you now in my longing for life to be good again. I love you here, Lord, in my soul's longings, desires, and heartaches. I consecrate to you my Primal Drive for Life. I surrender to you my ability to aspire for good things, plan for them, take hold of them, enjoy them, and keep on aspiring. I consecrate all living in me to you, Lord Jesus; I give you my famished craving for life to be good again. I love you*

here. I love you right here. And now I ask that the river of your life would flow in me, in my Primal Drive for Life and in my longing for life to be good again. I open my heart and soul to the river of life. Let it flow in me, through me, and all around me—restoring, renewing, and healing me. You alone are the life I seek, and I welcome your river into my heart and soul; I receive the river of your life in me. Thank you, God! In your mighty name I pray.

We are going to explore a number of "supernatural graces" as we move through this book. It will help your faith to know that your experience of these will be gentle. Though we call them "supernatural" graces, that doesn't mean they come like an earthquake or lightning strike. God is tender with our weary souls; he doesn't overwhelm us with his presence. As we practice these graces, their strength will grow. But your initial experience of them will be gentle—this will help you trust what you are experiencing.

Give this simple prayer, asking for the River of Life, a try for one week; you'll see.

LOST AND DISORIENTED

The first thing you should do when you are lost is stop! This is critical—
stop moving and get your bearings. Even if it takes some time. The classic
mistake of those who don't survive in crisis situations is that they panic
and run off in hopeless directions, or simply slog on, making their situa-
tion more dire.

In 1857 John Muir and a companion were caught in a blizzard on
the 14,142-foot summit of Mount Shasta, a volcanic peak in northern
California. No Gore-Tex, no down, no ice axes or storm tents.

> *After we had forced our way down the ridge and past the group*
> *of hissing fumaroles, the storm became inconceivably violent. The*
> *thermometer fell twenty-two degrees in a few minutes, and soon*
> *dropped below zero. The hail gave place to snow, and darkness*
> *came on like night. The wind, rising to the highest pitch of violence,*
> *boomed and surged amidst the desolate crags; lightning flashes*
> *in quick succession cut the gloomy darkness; and the thunders,*
> *the most tremendously loud and appalling I ever heard, made an*
> *almost continuous roar, stroke following stroke in quick, passionate*
> *succession, as though the mountain were being rent to its founda-*
> *tions and the fires of the old volcano were breaking forth again.*[1]

Muir, a seasoned mountaineer, had taken careful note of prominent
mountain features on their way to the summit, and he used those to guide
them safely—first to refuge on the mountain, and again the next morning
as they made their escape.

Chapter 2

Where Are We?
What's Happening?

When you see clouds beginning to form in the west,
you say, "Here comes a shower." And you are right.
When the south wind blows, you say, "Today will be a
scorcher." And it is. You fools! You know how to inter-
pret the weather signs of the earth and sky, but you
don't know how to interpret the present times.

LUKE 12:54–56 NLT

I remember the first time I got really and truly lost.

My young sons and I were elk hunting high in the
Rocky Mountains in Colorado. There'd been a decent
snowstorm the night before, and as we circumnavigated the
mountain, we could see the tracks of every living thing—not

only elk and deer but snowshoe hares, ermines, pine squir-rels, and field mice. I love reading the stories that footprints in fresh snow tell.

Then we came upon human tracks.

I was really upset. I thought we had this mountain to ourselves. *What are these jokers doing up here?* We sat there staring in disbelief at the footprints when slowly, slowly as the sun rose, it dawned on us—they were *our* footprints.

Which meant that we'd been going in circles when I was certain we'd been going in a straight line. I thought we were headed from point A to point B, where one of our buddies was going to pick us up in his four-wheel drive truck. Our tracks told a different story. I had no idea where we were.

The disorientation threw me off-balance for quite some time. *Where are we? How long have we been wandering in circles? What do we do now? Which direction is the way out?*

Our Perception Is Under Siege

I have nothing but compassion for you, dear beleaguered souls.

You really have nothing to compare this moment to, because this is the only hour in which you've ever lived. So it's only too easy to lose track of how soul-scorching and mind-numbing it is. And we are trying to process it all with trauma brain (what my friends refer to as "COVID brain").

Mental fragmentation is one of the classic symptoms fol-lowing trauma. Five minutes after brushing my teeth, I don't remember if I brushed my teeth. I pick up my phone to text someone, and in the four seconds it takes to raise my arm, I don't recall who I was going to text. I can't stay focused on one task very long; I flit from thing to thing.

Yesterday I walked up to our office doors and absent-mindedly tried to open them with my car's key fob. We have one of those systems where every employee has a fob on their key ring to open the front door. Only I was trying to open it with my *car* key fob (they don't look anything alike). I stood there puzzled, pressing *click-click-click*, and it was only when I heard my car door locks going up and down that I realized why the office door wouldn't open.

Mercy.

With our fragmented brains we are still trying to take in the same amount of media we were in 2018. We are the most plugged-in generation ever. *Ever.* In a moment like ours—so much media, news, and sensation bombarding us from every direction, plus all the opinions and counter-opinions and misinformation on social media—it's hard to maintain perspective. "To keep your head when all about you are losing theirs," as Kipling observed.[2]

Yesterday I listened to a special report on people who work all those consumer helplines—the 800 numbers you call when you need to know how to plug in your dryer or change your flight. Apparently these folks don't just have tough jobs. They work in abusive environments. Harassment, pressure, verbal abuse. Another injustice is exposed, which is really important. But the day before, it was an entirely different report or exposé on another injustice. The constant barrage of injustice and outrage overwhelms the soul. It clouds our perspective on what the story is right now.

Making matters worse, over the past decade many people have made social media their news source. It's where they turn for what's current, what's getting attention, what's happening in the world. We forget that social media companies are private companies held by private owners with strong personal opinions about what should and shouldn't get air time. Simply because the president or prime minister said it, or social media is shouting it, doesn't mean it's important or even true. But boy oh boy is it whipping a lot of people into a frenzy.

One of the first warnings Jesus gave us about living through such times was simply "don't freak out." "You will hear of wars and threats of wars, but don't panic" (Matthew 24:6 NLT) or "see that you are not frightened" (NASB1995).

Unflappable Jesus, the most level-headed guy ever, simply refused to get baited into any of the drama of his own day. And he urges us to be unflappable too. Jesus knew that everything was going to be shouting for our attention, trying to get us all "spun up." This injustice, that exposé. The message shouted at us from every side is, "Get upset! You really ought to be upset about this!"

It wears a soul down.

And there is a way out.

There Is Only One Story

The human brain processes information in the form of narrative. This is one more example of how deeply story is woven into the fabric of reality.[3]

Story is the way we orient ourselves in the world. Story is how we figure things out, bring order and meaning to the events around us. The story we hold to at any given time shapes our perceptions, hopes, and expectations; it gives us a place to stand. In this mad hour on the earth, what story are you telling yourself—or letting others tell you?

Is it a political narrative? *We just need to get the right people in power!*

Is it a social narrative? *The issue is injustice! We need justice!*

Is it about the economy? *A new era of prosperity is coming!*

Most importantly, is it the story God is telling?

We are living in a story, friends. A story written and being unfolded by the hand of God. Despite what the world is shouting at you, the story of God is still the story of the world. This is the hardest thing to hang on to, and the most important thing to hang on to: *the story of God is still the story of the world.*

Allow me to quote a passage from the book of Ephesians:

> God raised [Jesus] from death and set him on a throne in deep heaven, in charge of running the universe, everything from galaxies to governments, no name and no power exempt from his rule. And not just for the time being, but *forever*. He is in charge of it all, has the final word on everything. At the center of all this, Christ rules the church. The church, you see, is not peripheral to the world; the world is peripheral to the church. (Ephesians 1:20–23 THE MESSAGE)

Story is how we figure things out, bring order and meaning to the events around us. The story we hold to at any given time shapes our perceptions, hopes, and expectations; it gives us a place to stand.

Your current emotional state—does it reflect your confidence that Jesus is absolute Lord of everything on earth, galaxies to governments? That his church is center stage, not the world? That Christ is going to get the final word?

Yeah . . . me neither.

Honestly, Paul sounds deluded, like he's trying to convince himself the earth is flat.

Think about the sociopolitical scene when Paul was writing Ephesians, making bold statements like *Jesus is in charge of running the universe, no power exempt from his rule.* When he was going on like this, Christianity was nothing—it was a tiny little sect of a tiny ancient religious group in a forgotten corner of the Roman Empire. Rome was *the* story. From the north of Britain to the Middle East and North Africa, Rome ruled the Western world. It was described as "the most extensive political and social structure in Western civilization."[4] Israel was a tiny, conquered, subjugated country. Fragmented, impoverished, oppressed.

When they executed the man who some thought was the Messiah, it looked like the story of Rome was going to continue to be the story of the world for a very long time.

And where is that Roman Empire now?

Gone. Vanished. It fell within a couple hundred years after the writing of Ephesians. It was Christianity that kept growing for the next two thousand years, gaining vast global influence, reaching the four corners of the world.

Take another example—Genghis Khan, the Mongol leader in the thirteenth century. He actually ruled a larger land empire than Rome, the largest land empire in history. At their peak, the Mongols controlled an empire between eleven and twelve million contiguous square miles—an area about the size of Africa. Genghis Khan boasted of killing 10 percent of the world's population; he called himself "the Scourge of God."[5] If you were living at that time, Khan sure would have seemed like the Big Story. And where is all that now?

Where are the Beatles now? If you were living in the 1960s and early 1970s, the Beatles were *the* story. You couldn't read a paper or listen to the news without knowing what they'd worn that day, had for breakfast, if Paul had coughed or John had sneezed. And where are the Beatles now?

The story of God, the story of Jesus Christ has been, is now, and always will be the story of the world.

This is *so* important for the friends of God to keep in front of us; it's one of those things to put on a sticky note on your refrigerator or bathroom mirror: *the story of God has been, is now, and always will be the story of the world.*

Every human heart on this planet is beating because Jesus Christ is sustaining it. Every breath that every man, woman, and child will take in this moment, and then the next moment, and the next, they are being given because Jesus Christ is ruling everything.

The sun came up today; the sun will come up tomorrow, because Jesus Christ is actually ruling. Think of all the millions of beautiful things taking place in nature right now. The caribou are still migrating. The dolphins are still swimming in the oceans. Whales are still coming up for air, diving down deep. The whole animal kingdom is living, breathing, and flourishing because Jesus Christ is the story, and because he is sustaining all things by the power of his mighty word, as Hebrews 1:3 says.

Clinging to this fact will really help you "keep your head."

And This Story Is Racing Toward a Climax

When we were young, time seemed transcendent. A single summer felt like it would go on forever. As we mature, we come to realize that our days are a mere breath, and time races by as if it had a flight to catch. As if it were going somewhere.

It is.

Stories march toward a climax. I don't know why we fight this so hard.

We keep pushing off the future as if it weren't drawing nearer every single day. But stories are linear, moving forward in a firm direction, not circular. Life here as we know it does not go on forever; this great story is *hurtling* toward a climax. We are told to take this seriously, but we continue to suppress reality like a child who doesn't want to grow up.

Most people sense the tension of these times. They *feel* the instability—the shifting currents, polarization, governments reaching for more and more control, the cry for justice. But they don't go any further to get clarity. Something is in the air, a sense of imminence, but the world wants to pretend everything is fine, like a cancer patient who can't bring themself to face their diagnosis.

Honestly, it feels like the days and hours before Pearl Harbor.

There were warning signs of mounting Japanese aggression

as December 1941 drew near. Japan allied with Germany and Italy in 1940, and they began invading French-Indo China, British Malaysia, Singapore, Dutch Indonesia, and the Philippines. The US responded by freezing Japanese assets and petroleum shipments. We severed commercial and financial relations with Japan. Tensions were high. Warning signs continued; military code breakers were working round the clock.

But Honolulu in December 1941 was practically idyllic. The servicemen posted there enjoyed everything the islands had to offer—gorgeous beaches, lush fruits, umbrella drinks, the pulsing nightlife. Mentally, it's hard to believe you could be attacked when your adversary seems a million miles away and you're walking around paradise wearing flip-flops and drinking mai tais. Midnight on December 6 found most servicemen in the bars, dance clubs, walking with their girl on the beaches, or finishing a last drink at the Royal Hawaiian, where the officers hung out.

As the orchestra played "The Star-Spangled Banner" at the Royal Hawaiian hotel, Lieutenant Commander Edwin Layton, the Pacific fleet's intelligence officer, stood at attention alongside everyone else. Having absorbed weeks of disquieting reports about Japan's belligerent intentions and the probable imminence of war, he felt a wild urge to yell "Wake up, America!" Instead, he stood still and kept quiet.[6]

He kept quiet not because of fear, but simply because folks wouldn't believe him. But they were about to.

I simply want to point out that if you were living in Honolulu on the evening of December 6, 1941, wouldn't you have wanted advance warning on the story that was unfolding if you *could* have gotten it? Of course you would.

Our story is racing toward a climax, friends, just as every story does whether you want it to or not. Is this idea really that shocking?

Of Course We Are Nearing the End of the Age

Jesus seemed pretty frustrated at his contemporaries' refusal to understand their times. "Fools," he called them. Because knowing your moment *matters*. Knowing where you are in the story is critical for your survival. Every moment is *not* like another.

Living at the beginning of the *Lord of the Rings* is different from living at the end of the story. In the early stages we are in the happy Shire; we have an invitation to Bilbo's birthday party. But the story races on, picking up momentum toward the end where we find ourselves in the battle before the gates of Mordor—the great fight at the gates of hell itself. Do you see the difference and why Jesus wants you to know where you are?

The world keeps trying to get back to Bilbo's party, but the story doesn't stay there. No story does. You have to go *forward* to get to the party!

Look—the closest and dearest friends of Jesus thought the end of the age was drawing near:

> Dear children, this is the last hour. (1 John 2:18)

> The end of all things is near. Therefore be alert and of
> sober mind. (1 Peter 4:7)

You either have to write this off by thinking, *Well, those
guys were obviously wrong.* Or adopt a little humility and
start with the fact that the Scriptures are from God, that
Peter and John were speaking by inspiration of the Holy
Spirit, and maybe it is we who don't see clearly. It's quite
possible that their moment *was* the "last hour," and therefore we are in the last *seconds* of the age! There is good
reason to think so.

Now, this is not a book on prophecy. Some folks find
strength in prophecy. Most people are rather confused by it
and leave it for others to sort out. Nevertheless, there are clear
signs we ought to be paying attention to. One of the most
significant signs was given to us by Jesus in what is known as
the Olivet Discourse, where Christ laid out the signs of his
coming and his counsel for living through the end of the age:

> And this gospel of the kingdom will be preached in the
> whole world as a testimony to all nations, and then the
> end will come. (Matthew 24:14)

The gospel of Jesus Christ needs to reach every nation,
and then Christ will return. That's fairly straightforward;
that's a sign we can recognize. First this, then that.

Guess what—there's growing consensus among mis-
sionary leaders that every nation will have received the

testimony of the gospel in the next decade or two. This sign, given to us by Jesus himself, is about to be fulfilled. As the leader of a missions organization network reported,

> Even as recently as 2015, there were still more than 1,400 groups with no known Christians. But today, there are only a few hundred unengaged groups remaining, and hundreds of people groups are being engaged with the gospel each year. By God's grace . . . the church will reach all of the remaining groups by the end of 2022, or shortly thereafter. We're very close to the finish line.[7]

It's possible that by the time you read this sentence, the gospel will have reached all nations. That ought to get your attention! It isn't the only sign Christ gave us, but it's one of the most significant. Which means the promised return is near. Very near. I am not predicting dates, folks. I'm simply pointing out that the story of God is sweeping toward a climax.[*]

There Is No Zombie Apocalypse

However, as soon as we try to raise the possibility that God's story is approaching the end of the age that Scripture has so much to say about, most people get the heebie-jeebies.

I think their anxieties arise from a combination of vague, primal fears about whatever "the end" means, plus

---

[*] This isn't the only biblical prophecy that has come true, pointing toward the imminent return of Christ. The sudden, utterly unexpected re-formation of Israel as a nation in 1948 is another.

our urgent desire to get back to Bilbo's party, a desire made even more intense by trial or trauma. Honestly, I think many people would trade the return of Jesus Christ himself for a nice little end to their story and let another generation live through the end of the age.

We need to deal with those vague, primal fears because most of that stuff has been shaped by end-of-the-world movies rather than by the words of Jesus. Folks imagine the end of the age as some sort of postapocalyptic hour in which everyone is trying to kill one another in the streets with garden tools. And who wants to live through that? I get it. But is that what Jesus told us to expect?

> When the Son of Man returns, it will be like it was in Noah's day. In those days, the people enjoyed banquets and parties and weddings right up to the time Noah entered his boat and the flood came and destroyed them all. And the world will be as it was in the days of Lot. People went about their daily business—eating and drinking, buying and selling, farming and building—until the morning Lot left Sodom. Then fire and burning sulfur rained down from heaven and destroyed them all. Yes, it will be "business as usual" right up to the day when the Son of Man is revealed. (Luke 17:26–30 NLT)

Buying and selling, farming and building require economic stability. The world is not going to be hurled into some massive economic chaos where we are trading our car for a loaf of bread. That's not what Jesus said. Banquets, parties, and weddings require social and cultural stability.

People throw parties when the neighborhood is safe and happy, not huddled in the basement.

Folks, there is no zombie apocalypse. Repeat that with me—*there is no zombie apocalypse.*

In fact, everything Jesus said about his sudden return to this planet assumes the element of *surprise.* Life is going to look and feel like business as usual until the moment the archangel blows the trumpet and God himself steps in to sweep away evil and start the joy!

Now yes—Jesus also said those final days will be times of great testing, and that's the part folks don't like. I understand. But if we have been given the honor of being assigned to those days, wouldn't you want to know? Wouldn't you want to prepare your heart, soul, mind, and strength?

If we aren't in those days, we are certainly standing on the precipice. Even if you think, *Perhaps Christ may return in my children's lifetime, or my grandchildren's,* that hour is so close to this moment, in terms of biblical history, you are living at the end of the age, dear one.

What Am I Supposed to Do?

The first thing called for is mental resilience; we have to keep our heads. It's almost shocking when we realize how spun up we've been. "Don't freak out" is essentially what Jesus was saying. This advice is drilled into every form of military training and survival course—when things get hot, don't freak out. Keep your cool so you can make good decisions.

It would be wise to get your bearings right now:

- If this isn't the end of the age, we're on the edge of it.
- This is a very trying time.
- I need to take my resilience much more seriously.

I'll say more about cultivating mental resilience later in the book, but a simple, satisfying step is to get your head out of the "wars and rumors of wars" and back into the story God is telling. For example: the story of God should get more of your "attention time" than any other media.

If you spend thirty minutes a day consuming what is called news (this includes all social media), then you need to spend *more* than thirty minutes—maybe twice as much—in the Scriptures or listening to biblical podcasts. Instead of using your downtime to scroll through Facebook or Instagram, use it to read something that reminds you of the story of God—a psalm, a good sermon, even a simple quote.

Remember—the battle right now is for the narrative; who gets to frame the story for you? Either it will be God, or someone else. If you are "alarmed," something has drawn your attention away from the story of God. Let your fears, anxieties, anger, or rage alert you that you've been taken hostage; stop and get your bearings.

A friend of mine got completely addicted to the news during the 2020 pandemic and US presidential election (which was full of drama). He realized how upset he had become from the daily consumption, so he quit. Cold turkey. He walked away from the news for six months. You might think that irresponsible, but Jesus gave us a simple test: you shall know them by their fruit. The fruit of the media consumption was stress, anger, depression, and rage.

The story of God should get
more of your "attention time"
than any other media.

The fruit of walking away? In my friend's own words, "I have more peace and joy in my life now than I ever have."

Skill
KEEPING GOD'S PERSPECTIVE

Read this reflection on Psalm 23 out loud to yourself.

The Lord is my shepherd, I lack nothing.

Jesus is still in charge, still deeply involved in my life and world—guiding, leading, providing.

He makes me lie down in green pastures,
he leads me beside quiet waters,
he refreshes my soul.

God restores my weary heart; he gives me resilience . . . if I follow him.

He guides me along the right paths
for his name's sake.

Don't get baited into all the sociodrama; let God lead me each and every day.

Even though I walk
through the darkest valley,
I will fear no evil,
for you are with me;
your rod and your staff,
they comfort me.

Yes, we are in a dark time. But God is still protecting me and comforting me. I am not navigating this on my own.

You prepare a table before me
in the presence of my enemies.
You anoint my head with oil;
my cup overflows.

God has a feast of goodness for me even in rough times; he fills my famished craving.

Surely your goodness and love will follow me
all the days of my life,
and I will dwell in the house of the Lord
forever.

My reality is not determined by pandemics, politics, or any-thing else. I live in God; he lives in me. His goodness is with me today, and my future is absolutely wonderful.

Maybe you should tape this to the fridge and say it out loud every day.

DO NOT GIVE UP!

One of the great dangers of hypothermia is that when you are in the late stages you become sleepy and simply want to lie down and drift away into unconscious bliss. But to do so is to die. To prevent this Muir and his companion weathered that blizzard on Mount Shasta by lying down, completely exposed to the elements, on top of the gas vents and fumaroles of the volcanic mountain.

> *When the heat became unendurable, on some spot where steam was escaping through the sludge, we tried to stop it with snow and mud, or shifted a little at a time by shoving with our heels; for to stand in blank exposure to the fearful wind in our frozen-and-broiled condition seemed certain death. . . .*
>
> *The frost grew more and more intense, and we became icy and covered over with a crust of frozen snow, as if we had lain cast away in the drift all winter. In about thirteen hours—every hour like a year—day began to dawn, but it was long ere the summit's rocks were touched by the sun. . . .*
>
> *As the time drew near to make an effort to reach camp, we became concerned to know what strength was left us, and whether or no we could walk; for we had lain flat all this time without once rising to our feet. Mountaineers, however, always find in themselves a reserve of power after great exhaustion. It is a kind of second life, available only in emergencies like this; and, having proved its existence, I had no great fear that either of us would fail, though one of my arms was already benumbed and hung powerless.[1]*

Chapter 3

The Strength That Prevails

Keep alert at all times. And pray that you might be strong
enough to escape . . . and stand before the Son of Man.
LUKE 21:36 NLT

I think everyone prays at some point in their life, even if they're not sure someone is listening. And I'll bet that one of the most common prayers goes something like, *Lord help me; give me strength.*

I really like that prayer. It has a genuine humility to it. We find ourselves facing something that overwhelms our personal resources, and we cry out for help, for strength. The man who casually answers his phone on a Tuesday afternoon only to hear that his family has been killed in an automobile accident. The woman who, at a routine exam, learns she has Stage IV breast cancer. The caregiver who day after day labors under the crushing load of providing for every need of their incapacitated loved one.

Give me strength, Lord.

Jesus liked that prayer.

He instructed us to pray it, and he prayed it himself.[2]

Toward the end of his days on earth, he began to give his disciples clear instructions for living through extremely hard times, knowing they would record those instructions for future generations—including you, dear ones. He assured us in no uncertain terms that this story would sweep toward a climax, and that those days would be especially hard on the human soul. He urged us to ask for the strength that prevails:

> Notice the fig tree, or any other tree. When the leaves come out, you know without being told that summer is near. In the same way, when you see all these things taking place, you can know that the Kingdom of God is near. I tell you the truth, this generation will not pass from the scene until all these things have taken place. Heaven and earth will disappear, but my words will never disappear. Watch out! Don't let your hearts be dulled by carousing and drunkenness, and by the worries of this life. Don't let that day catch you unaware, like a trap. For that day will come upon everyone living on the earth. Keep alert at all times. And pray that you might be strong enough to escape these coming horrors and stand before the Son of Man. (Luke 21:29–36 NLT)

Strong enough to escape—that's who and what we want to be. Strong enough to be the survivors, the triumphant ones. To make it through the storm.

This is no ordinary strength Jesus is offering. This isn't

optimism, this isn't simply feeling refreshed for a new day. Hard times require something more than willpower. Jesus warns us, urges us, practically commands us to ask for strength. The Greek word used here is *katischuó* and it means

> to be strong to another's detriment;
> to prevail against;
> to be superior in strength;
> to overcome;
> to prevail.[3]

This is a valiant strength. It implies a fight, an enemy we can and will prevail over. It reminds me of Henry V's prayer on the eve of the battle of Agincourt. The English troops are exhausted; many are wounded or ill. They face a fresh French army five times their size, fighting on their home turf. Henry's men are overwhelmed. He falls to his knees in the darkness and prays for strength:

> O God of battles, steel my soldiers' hearts.
> Possess them not with fear; take from them
>   now
> The sense of reckoning, if the opposed
>   numbers
> Pluck their hearts from them.[4]

He cries out to the God of war. You understand, I hope, that our English translation "Lord Almighty" is correctly translated "Lord of heaven's *armies*." Our God is the God of war, "mighty in battle" (Psalm 24:8). We need him to strengthen our hearts so we are as protected as if by steel, as *immovable* as steel.

There is only one other time the word *katischuó* is used in the New Testament. Jesus is again the speaker, and he pronounces the coming victory of his newly launched movement, the revolution that is the church triumphant. Matthew records this moment for us; Jesus promises that the forces of hell will *not* "prevail against" (NKJV) or "overcome" his church: "And I also say to you that you are Peter, and upon this rock I will build My church; and the gates of Hades will not overpower it" (Matthew 16:18 NASB).

This is no coincidence that *katischuó* is used only in these two verses. Jesus wants us to understand that it is the powers of hell that are trying to overpower us, to crush the human heart—especially the hearts of his followers. The strength God urges us to ask for is a combative strength, a strength to win the fight, to overcome. Wouldn't that be wonderful right now?

We need strength of heart, strength of mind, strength of spirit. A strength that prevails. Because there are forces urging us to quit.

The Temptation Is to Give Up

"I know I should get out. I know exercise is good for my body, but I just don't want to do anything."

I was talking to a dear young woman who was wrestling with the early stages of depression. Part of it was due to the pandemic trauma—that was her vulnerability. The better part of it was coming from an attack of the enemy that had come over her in her weakened condition. "I know seeing people is good for me too. But I just want to lie on the couch. I don't have the strength to do the things I know would help me right now."

I left thinking to myself, *How do we find the strength to prevail when we don't even want to ask for it?*

A few days later I was sitting in the woods by a lovely, small brook. The day was hot and the shade of the evergreens was delightful, made even more refreshing by the coolness and the song of the brook. I sat down on the mossy bank and just let the healing power of this little Eden wash over my tired body and soul. I was thinking about my friend and about my own struggles to keep faith.

After about fifteen minutes my attention was caught by the spiders that were weaving their webs over the brook itself. I was baffled by their architectural brilliance—how can they string their first web strands over a running brook? It must be pure acrobatics. Their webs stretched a quarter of an inch above the water's surface—the perfect place to catch mosquitoes, gnats, and such flying up and down the rivulet.

And there the spiders sat and waited, perfectly still. I was amazed at their patience, waiting for days motionless, undetected, to catch one prey. I suddenly thought of our enemy—how he will set up cultural schemes and snares that take years to play out in order to trap humanity.

The era we just lived through—what I would call the Comfort Culture—weakened us for the trials we are facing.

Before there was any pandemic, universities were reporting that their mental health services were being overwhelmed by freshmen within the first few weeks of a new year, primarily with issues of anxiety and depression. The director of a program designed to prepare freshmen for the college years told me recently, "Eighteen is the new twelve. Our students are emotionally underdeveloped. They're much less resilient than any we've ever encountered, and I'm not entirely sure why."

There are many reasons, of course; human beings are beautifully complicated. But honestly, when you grow up in a world where everything is done with a few clicks on your phone, it doesn't exactly develop resilience. Anyone living in the developed world has experienced a level of ease unimaginable to previous generations. This is the overnight delivery age. Let me be quick to say, I have fully enjoyed all the conveniences of our modern moment. But I'm also aware that they've made me soft. The web we have been caught in was years in the making—a brilliant interlacing of the Comfort Culture and the Babel of technology at our fingertips.* By way of contrast, the World War II generation emerged from the Great Depression with a sense of reality, grit, and resilience.

The pandemic was an apocalypse in the true meaning of the word—it *revealed* many things about us and our world. We don't like much of what it uncovered, including the fact

---

* If you've seen Bo Burnham's music video "Welcome to the Internet," you know exactly what I mean. His documentary of his solo journey into depression during quarantine is deeply disturbing because it reveals what we are all facing.

When you grow up in a world where everything is done with a few clicks on your phone, it doesn't exactly develop resilience.

that we are not as resilient as we thought we were when things were going smoothly.

So we come into this really tough moment in a compromised state. It's like being dropped into the war in Afghanistan barefoot, and you have the flu. We've been set up for this loss of heart, set up to be overcome, set up to give in. Jesus knew all this, and lovingly told us to ask for the strength that prevails. There's an urgency to his voice.

Here's why.

The Falling Away

Giving up has always been a struggle for frail humanity. But when Jesus urges us to ask for strength to *escape*, he has something particular in mind, something he sees coming: "At that time many will turn away from the faith" (Matthew 24:10).

Saint Paul was deeply troubled by this as he wrote his friends living in Thessalonica: "Let no one deceive you by any means; for that Day [the day Christ returns] will not come unless the falling away comes first" (2 Thessalonians 2:3 NKJV). Prior to the climax of this story, and the wonderful return of Jesus to make everything new, there will be some sort of global Falling Away. The Greek word here is *apostasia*, and that is why some translations put it this way: "No one is to deceive you in any way! For it will not come unless the apostasy comes first" (2 Thessalonians 2:3 NASB).

But the word *apostasy* conjures up more zombie apocalypse imagery, and that's not helpful in our effort to understand our situation. I don't think we're going to see millions of people tattooing "I hate God; I love Satan" on their chests, or marches in every major city blaspheming Jesus Christ. Satan is much cleverer than all that. I believe what we will see—what we see happening now—is simply people giving up on God in large numbers. Which is why I think the New Life Version has it right: "For the Lord will not come again until many people turn away from God" (2 Thessalonians 2:3).

The stories first began to come into our ministry by ones and twos—we'd hear of a famous worship leader or an acquaintance from church who'd walked away from their faith. In the past twelve months the evidence grew in larger numbers. Mature believers, once so passionate for Christ, had either blown up their lives or simply slipped away, giving up on God. Of course, the politics around COVID split many churches, but lots of those folks didn't find a new congregation—they just stayed home. Angry partisan politics done in the name of Jesus turned many people off to the faith of their youth. Many have migrated to a more culturally acceptable faith, forsaking the difficult truths of Christianity for something easier to associate with.

I believe we may be witnessing the Great Falling Away.

Let me be quick to say that there isn't a simple explanation nor simplistic solution. Some people are fed up with religion. But much of the turning from God is born out of heartache and disappointment—God did not seem to help. He did not seem to hear. These are the deepest hurts of the human heart. We will explore what to do with those hurts as we go along, but let me say here that giving up your faith is like finding yourself in a desert, your weary legs throbbing with pain. You can't find your way out by cutting your legs off. God can handle your anger, disappointment, even bitterness. But walking away from Jesus is forsaking your only hope out of the heartache.

I bring this up because the enemy is wickedly skilled at pouncing on our vulnerabilities. He is using these trying times to cloud our hearts with unbelief. If in fact the Falling Away is sweeping the earth, we want to have advance warning. It gets in the air like poison, and we don't want to slowly succumb to it ourselves. It gains a social momentum, and since we are social creatures, we can get swept up in it without a conscious decision on our part.

The pandemic put us all in a heightened state of longing for life to be good again. We rushed out to make that happen in some way, shape, or form. But every such effort disappoints; even the most fabulous vacation is not going to heal your soul from trauma. We return to a world still filled with tension and fear. Disillusionment sets us up for a serious loss of heart. We give up on God because we feel he hasn't come through.

This is exactly what the enemy has planned all along.

But this is our moment, and Jesus offers us strength, so let us seize it now with both hands while we still can.

It Begins with a Choice

I have counseled thousands of men and women, and I can tell you with utter confidence—both from their experiences and my own—that whatever else the enemy brings against you, he will always bring with it a feeling of *I don't want to fight this*. This feeling is called *ennui*, a weariness of spirit, a malaise, that sense of *I just don't want to fight anymore*. This is Kierkegaard's sickness unto death, by which he meant "intensified doubt, super-doubt, mega-doubt."[5]

And this feeling is not your true heart.

Friends, this is so helpful to understand: that weariness you're feeling, that *Not now; maybe later*, that sense of being overwhelmed, that *Why bother? Who cares?*—this is the enemy, not you. When you know that, you're much better prepared against it. You can more clearly choose to resist. *I reject this feeling of* Why bother? Who cares? *and I reject this feeling that I don't even want to fight. I do! I choose the strength that prevails! I don't want to be one of those folks who get taken out at the end.*

Some people seem born with a greater measure of resilience. John Muir certainly was. He would leave camp before dawn with nothing more than a hunk of bread in his pocket and hike for thirty miles. The Comfort Culture doesn't exactly foster that kind of physical and mental toughness!

But resilience is also something that is *bestowed*, something *imparted* by God into our frail humanity. That's truly good news.

> "My strength is gone," [Daniel said,] "and I can hardly breathe." Again the one who looked like a man touched me and gave me strength. "Do not be afraid, you who are highly esteemed," he said. "Peace! Be strong now; be strong." When he spoke to me, I was strengthened. (Daniel 10:17–19)

Resilience is also something that is *bestowed*, something *imparted* by God into our frail humanity. That's truly good news.

The first fruit of katischuó is the ability to not give up. It imbues us with that Churchillian grit: *Never surrender; never give up!* The strength that prevails—this mighty, combative warrior-strength—first comes to us simply as the strength not to quit. Because when you're tired, when you're beat up, you just want relief—a bag of chips, a bottle of wine, to lie on the couch and binge on Netflix. Jesus urges us to be on our guard, "so that your hearts will not be weighed down. . . . praying that you will have strength to escape all these things" (Luke 21:34, 36 NASB).

Jesus says there is a means of escape. Wouldn't you love an escape from all the madness? Okay then—let's make the choice right now to *receive* it.

Skill
RECEIVING THE STRENGTH THAT PREVAILS

How do we tap into katischuó, the strength that prevails?

It starts with what I like to call being single-hearted. We are single-hearted when we cherish God above all things. We love him in the longing for relief, which is where we are vulnerable. We love him in the longing for life to be good again. Scripture promises that God will come to the help of those who are single-hearted: "The eyes of the LORD search the whole earth in order to strengthen those whose hearts are fully committed to him" (2 Chronicles 16:9 NLT).

God gives the strength that prevails to those whose hearts are fully given over to him. This is why it's so important to stay single-hearted. Notice that before offering the strength that prevails, Jesus urged us to turn from the things that seem to offer life but wear us down: "Watch out! Don't let your hearts be dulled by carousing and drunkenness, and by the worries of this life. Don't let that day catch you unaware, like a trap" (Luke 21:34–35 NLT).

Now, Jesus enjoyed a glass of wine himself, so why did he especially name drinking here? There's a kind of drinking that is *surrender*; nearly everyone who drinks knows what I'm talking about. You get home at the end of the day utterly beat up and worn out, and you just want to "have a glass and veg." This isn't the drink of joy, the toast at a wedding, the dinner with comrades. This is the little white flag of surrender.

Saint John of the Cross, whose story I shared in chapter 1, was single-hearted. When his captors beat him mercilessly and then offered him his freedom if he would renounce his allegiance to Christ, he refused. God gave this single-hearted man the strength that prevails.

As we turn our hearts toward Jesus or our Father (they are one), we practice loving him. *I love you, God. I love you, God. I love you, God.* This is not *feeling* love; the warfare and the weariness will often make you feel rather blank. We choose to love God anyways. This is the strength that prevails, giving you the first step of courage to stand and be single-hearted. Over and over again we practice loving God. *I love you, Lord.*

And we ask him for katischuó—his overcoming, prevailing, conquering strength. God offers it, so ask, ask, ask!

Father, Jesus, Holy Spirit—God of all creation, God of the thunderstorm and the waterfall, I need your strength. I need the strength that prevails. I don't want to fall away; I don't want to lose heart. I choose you above all things. I give you my allegiance and my undivided love. I choose single-heartedness toward you, Lord Jesus—body, soul, and spirit; heart, mind, and will. I pray for a supernatural resilience, God. Fill me with your overcoming strength, a victorious strength. Father, Lord of heaven and earth, strengthen me. I pray for strength of mind, strength of heart, strength of will. I pray for the strength that allows me to escape all that is coming against the saints in this hour. Fill me with resilience. By faith I receive it and thank you for it. In Jesus' name, amen.

Beautiful. If I were you, I'd consider making this prayer something you turn to frequently. I've included all of these prayers in the back of the book so that you can easily access them. I've also developed an experience to accompany the practices in this book called "30 Days to Resilience," which I think you'll find immensely helpful. You can access it in my "One Minute Pause" app available for free in the App Store!

Everything else we explore and learn in this book will deepen our ability to receive the strength that prevails, along with more beautiful resources from God.

PREDATORS

The world is a dangerous place.

This startling fact sharpened the humility and wits of every generation prior to ours. But we live in the gourmet latte generation. The instant-information, overnight-delivery generation. When you return to reality by simply stepping one mile into nature, you are taken back into a world designed to make you a smart, resilient human being.

Not everyone learns those lessons.

Timothy Treadwell was a bear enthusiast, self-styled environmentalist, and documentary filmmaker. He "lived among" coastal brown bears—which he called grizzly bears—in Katmai National Park in Alaska for thirteen summers. Treadwell claims he was protecting bears from poachers, though park rangers report there had never been a recorded incident of poaching at Katmai. In 2003 Timothy lingered in Katmai into October with his girlfriend, although he usually left the park at the end of summer. By staying into fall, he put himself among new bears that had come down from the mountains—bears unaccustomed to his presence. Fall is also the time bears become aggressive and predatory as they store up calories for hibernation through winter. Treadwell and his girlfriend were killed and eaten by a twenty-eight-year-old coastal brown bear.

Some people called Timothy brave; others felt he was uniquely sensitive. Most Alaskans thought he was simply a crackpot. Whatever conclusion you come to watching Grizzly Man, a documentary on Treadwell's life and death, you cannot deny that he was truly, tragically naive.

Chapter 4

Eden Glory, Not Desolation

---

*Let no one deceive you by any means; for that Day will
not come unless the falling away comes first.*
2 THESSALONIANS 2:3 NKJV

Y ou've probably seen one of those nature documentaries
at some point in your life—magnificent cinematog-
raphy showing thousands of caribou migrating across the
tundra, or wildebeest making their annual pilgrimage across
the Serengeti.

Sweeping down from high above, the camera first shows
us a myriad of animals all moving in a vast wave, then zooms
in closer to discover a small member of the herd lagging
behind as the narrator explains, "The injured calf is now
dangerously separated from the herd." You don't even need
to guess what's coming next. Wolves. Hyenas. I hate that
part about nature; the world can be a violent place.

Jesus knows that very well, personally.

The urgency with which he sometimes pleads, urges, and warns us is born out of a profound sobriety. Wander away from your Shepherd and you will encounter harm. The forces of darkness come "to steal and kill and destroy" as he bluntly put it (John 10:10). Oh that we would take this more seriously than we do. What would the camera show if it panned down over our lives today to reveal what is stalking us?

I guarantee you we would move closer to our Shepherd.

But in our weary condition we just want flip-flops and mai tais, so we don't pay careful enough attention.

As Jesus began to explain the trials of the final hours, the urgency of his warnings increased:

You will be hated by everyone because of me, but the one who stands firm to the end will be saved. (Matthew 10:22)

The one who stands firm to the end will be saved. (Matthew 24:13)

By your endurance you will gain your lives. (Luke 21:19 ESV)

Endurance—the dividing line between those who make it through any sort of trial and those who don't.

Hang on, don't get discouraged—this isn't just gutting it out. Not at all. The beautiful resilience Jesus offers us comes from *his* resources; endurance is *imparted* to us. So let me pause and talk about being amphibians, creatures that can live in two worlds.

The Supernatural Graces

Christians are designed to live in and enjoy the benefits of two ecosystems, two realities—the physical and the spiritual, the earth and the heavens.

Each world offers graces for human flourishing. The natural world is saturated with beauty, and beauty nourishes the human soul. That's why we vacation in lovely places—when we're looking to be renewed, we choose walks in the woods, swimming in the ocean, biking through vineyards, music, and dinner on the patio under the stars. There are many natural graces that nourish and strengthen the heart and soul—beauty is one, stillness is another, and so are nature and disentangling from technology, but I wrote about those in a book released just before the pandemic, so I won't go into them here.[1]

We are also created to live comfortably in the *spiritual* world, to draw upon the supernatural graces available to us through the rest of God's wonderful kingdom.

If you've ever experienced the comfort of God, or the love of God, that was heaven coming to you here on earth. You tapped into the rest of God's kingdom for the help, strength, and sustenance you needed.

Prayer is reaching into the heavens for what we need. If you have had the joy of hearing Jesus speak to you, if he brings to you scriptures, songs, things that stir your heart, that's the heavens coming into your natural world. You are tapping into the resources of God's kingdom. And there is *so* much more to discover!

For some reason I'm thinking of penguins. They

If you've ever experienced

the comfort of God, or the

love of God, that was heaven

coming to you here on earth.

aren't technically amphibians, but they move comfortably between two worlds. Like most mammals that live on land—they nest on land, sleep on land, mate on land, raise their chicks on land. But they are wonderfully adept in the ocean. Penguins are, in fact, awkward on land, but they are so graceful, even elegant, as they swim and dive in the water. We are meant to be the same: not only adept but even elegant in our ability to swim in the rest of God's kingdom.

Our created nature is designed to live in two worlds, drawing our strength from two worlds; that's why I call us amphibians. But most of us are not tapping into the supernatural graces. We can't ignore these and hope to thrive in an hour like this one. If you place a frog—a true amphibian—in a tank of water with no dry place to crawl onto, it will die. If you place it in a terrarium with no water, it will die. Amphibians need both realms to thrive. We cannot hope to find resilience while we ignore the provision God has for us in the fullness of his beautiful kingdom.

Desolation

I suffered a couple of devastating emotional blows in the summer of 2021. There were things I felt God had promised me that, in heartbreaking ways, did not come through. I felt so betrayed, so abandoned. But then, in my vulnerable state, something came over me—a dark cloud, a sort of suffocating fog that urged me to give up my life with God.

I shared my experience with two colleagues of mine, godly men with a long history of relationship with Jesus. They confided that they, too, had experienced something exactly like my Desolation. In fact, both of them had gone through an episode in the spring of 2021 where they felt that they might entirely lose their faith. Given their resilience, I was shocked. It seemed absurd that such solid men of faith could come to that place.

What's important about all three of our stories is that once each of us came out from under this fog, and our life with God was back to normal. Everything was fine again. While there were genuine human disappointments involved, the sudden onset and dramatic relief from this fog revealed that it was from the enemy, tied directly to the Falling Away predicted for this hour (see chapter 3). The common symptom was a Desolation of heart and soul, which sure seems tied to something Jesus warned us about.

The prophet Daniel foretold a day when "the one who makes desolate" would step onto the world stage (Daniel 9:27 NASB). This was prophesied as part of the final trials of the age. Jesus then referred to this same reality in his own warning and counsels that we have been drawing from. Paul went on to link this force—whatever it may be—to the Falling Away he spoke of in 2 Thessalonians.

We don't need to get into labyrinthine debates over the Antichrist, the Beast, the whore of Babylon, and how all that might play out on the world stage. There's no need to go down that rabbit hole to simply acknowledge that something or someone is going to cause Desolation, and that Desolation is part of what causes people to give up on God. This is something we most definitely want to strengthen our hearts against. My colleagues and I have experienced it, and we've seen it in our clients and constituents around the world.

The symptoms include a sort of dullness of heart, a poverty of spirit, a barrenness of soul. Disappointment, so understandable given the circumstances, collapses into disillusionment. Neither hope nor joy comes easily.

Worst of all there comes a kind of blankness in our life with God. Faith feels flat, or dumb, or simply . . . gone. We are disappointed with God, and we feel we don't believe in him anymore. Hopelessness infects our faith. Like the limping caribou, we're beat up and lagging behind, vulnerable to the predators that want to drag our souls into Desolation. Trust me—you do not want to fall prey to this. It's terrible.

We must find the supernatural graces to guard our hearts against both Desolation, whatever the source, and the riptide pull to draw away from God—or even to give up on God entirely.

Because the battle is over the heart, my friends. Always. The battle is over your heart.

The Temple of Your Heart

What's fascinating is that this Desolation, whatever it may be, is linked in the Scriptures to defiling the temple of God. Because of this, many Christians assume that the temple in Jerusalem needs to be rebuilt for these last-days prophecies to come true.

But folks, have we forgotten that God relocated the temple? In a stunning shift of geography, God changed the playing field. He moved the temple from a physical building to the hearts of his people:

> Don't you know you yourselves are God's temple and that God's Spirit dwells in your midst? (1 Corinthians 3:16)

> God's temple is sacred, and you together are that temple. (1 Corinthians 3:17)

> For we are the temple of the living God. (2 Corinthians 6:16)

> Do you not know that your bodies are temples of the Holy Spirit, who is in you, whom you have received from God? (1 Corinthians 6:19)

You, dear child of God, follower of Jesus, are now the temple. The New Testament makes that clear. Follow this closely, because it is so very holy, so deeply encouraging, and it will bring you vital resilience for this hour. Your heart is the dwelling place of the Almighty! (If you've invited him in, which is easy to do. You simply say, "Lord Jesus—I need you. I really do. I open the temple of my heart to you; I ask you to come and dwell within me. I surrender my life to you in every way. Come and be my saving God, dwelling in my heart.")

In the Old Testament first came the tabernacle and then the temple. These were holy places where God came to be among his people:

Then the cloud covered the tent of meeting, and the glory of the LORD filled the tabernacle. (Exodus 40:34)

Then the temple of the LORD was filled with the cloud . . . for the glory of the LORD filled the temple. (2 Chronicles 5:13–14)

No wonder Satan tried on *multiple* occasions to defile, desecrate, and ultimately destroy both tabernacle and temple—for here was the epicenter of the life of Israel with their saving God. Here God met with his people.

But at the coming of Jesus Christ—Immanuel, God with us—the abiding place of the Holy One shifted in a breathtaking way. When Christ died upon the cross, the veil of the temple in Jerusalem was torn top to bottom; the Holy Spirit came down on Pentecost; and now the temple has moved location to the human heart, because that is where God comes to dwell "that Christ may dwell in your hearts" (Ephesians 3:17).*

The Desolation I described above and the Falling Away I laid out in chapter 3 make sense when we realize that our enemy knows God has set up a new temple—the heart of his people. So he tries to bring Desolation there. Satan is trying to defile the hearts of God's followers, because this is where the holy of holies now lies. (Here on earth, anyways; there is the true place in heaven.†)

---

* To explore the truth that the Christian is the temple of God, go to www.bibleproject.com and search their great resources on "temple." The more you understand the truth of this, the more you will be able to receive God's glory in you.

† This may help some Christians understand the nearness of the last days

We have seen this Desolation unfolding in the lives of thousands of people, and that is why I want to help you today. A friend once wrote to me about his experience with Desolation:

> I was asking Jesus more about that early this morning. He showed me a wasteland and said, "This is what Desolation wants to bring to the human heart." I'm seeing the idea is to bring emptiness and no hope. It's a great next move of the enemy coming off all of the trauma of the last year and a half. Malaise, compromise, isolation . . . but it's elusive and tough to nail down.

One Recent Example

One of the infamous consequences of COVID is the loss of taste and smell. For some people this symptom carries on for many, many months. The daughter of a friend of ours is a bright, musical, vibrant fifteen-year-old who, like her family, loves fantastic foods from around the world. Her particular favorite is Korean food. But she lost her sense of taste with COVID and *one year later* still hasn't gotten it back. She lost the joy of eating. Now, anyone can handle that for a week or two, but when it goes on for a year, it feels like

---

if they have until now believed that the Jewish temple in Jerusalem needed to be rebuilt and the sacrificial system reinstated for the Abomination to do his thing. In the new covenant period, the location of the temple clearly shifts to the human heart. It's something to consider. But you don't need to accept this as a possible interpretation to realize that we need to strengthen our hearts against our enemy, especially in trying times.

it will go on forever. This is such vulnerable territory, a place where Desolation can get in and take root.

We still don't know the long-term effects of all this, but it looks like up to a third of all cases are long-haul COVID, lasting more than six months.[2] I've had friends whose symptoms lasted more than a year. This wears down whatever remaining resilience we may have, making us vulnerable to Desolation in many forms—especially disappointment with God and pulling away from him.

Laura van Dernoot Lipsky is the founder and director of the Trauma Stewardship Institute. "Lipsky has spent decades helping people navigate the consequences of natural disasters, mass shootings, and other crises," wrote Ed Yong. "'As hard as the initial trauma is,' she said, 'it's the aftermath that destroys people.'"[3]

This is the coming storm I am most concerned about. Every therapist I know in the US and Europe has a long waiting list; this is the mental health crisis catching up with us. God our Father knew we were going to have to live through such times, and he has made provision for us.

Eden Glory

When you think of what Desolation looks like, picture a barren desert. Desolation wants to make everything a wasteland.

So what is the opposite of a wasteland?

Eden! The paradise of God, our first home, with all its lush, glorious beauty overflowing here, there, everywhere!

God our Father knew we were going to have to live through such times, and he has made provision for us.

If you follow the flow of Scripture and human history, you can see that our enemy wants to make everything a wasteland, and God wants to make everything a restored Eden. When it comes to the resilience we need against Desolation, part of our Father's provision is his Eden Glory—the glory of God in you and around you, giving you supernatural resilience and guarding you like a shield.

What do I mean by Eden Glory?

Think of the wedding at Cana, where Jesus turned water into wine. Christ had the attendants fill six stone jars with water. Each jar could hold up to thirty gallons. Then Jesus turned every drop into wine—and fine, sumptuous wine at that, the kind of wine you'd expect to find in Eden, or at the wedding feast of the Lamb! One hundred eighty gallons of exquisite wine poured into the party at the end of the evening. (Jesus is the kind of person you want to hang out with, by the way; he knows how to bring joy to any occasion!)

After telling that story, John wrote, "What Jesus did here in Cana of Galilee was the first of the signs through which he revealed his glory; and his disciples believed in him" (John 2:11).

What exactly did Jesus reveal? God's supernatural power to overcome shortage and deprivation with overwhelming abundance! That's his glory; he did it by the power of his glory.

In the book of Romans, Paul is trying to help us understand the availability of the power of God for us, in us. He turned to the resurrection and said, "Just as Christ was raised from the dead through the glory of the Father, we too may live a new life" (Romans 6:4). It was by the glory of God that Jesus was raised from the dead. The glory of God—the regenerative, resurrecting Eden Glory of God.

Isaiah reminds us that "the whole earth is full of his glory" (Isaiah 6:3). Think of the sun, how absolutely wonderful the sun is! Its radiance, beauty, and cheerfulness, and how much life it gives! It is pulsating with the glory-power of God. Think of the oceans and the forests of the world, how vast they are, how filled with life. The whole world is filled with the glory of God. It is the life-giving, life-sustaining, *generative power* of God.

So, for our purposes here, when you think of the glory of God, think of the sun, the ocean, water turned into wine, Christ raised from the dead. Think of Eden.

Now for something truly breathtaking: you are meant to be filled with the glory of God.

Think back to the tabernacle and temple—in the Old Testament, the glory of the Lord filled the tabernacle, then the temple. The manifest presence of God came and dwelt there, filled with radiance, beauty, and regenerative power. And where is the temple now? You are the temple. The New Testament makes that clear. This is why Paul wrote,

> But we all, with unveiled faces, looking as in a mirror at the glory of the Lord, are being transformed into the same image from glory to glory, just as from the Lord, the Spirit. (2 Corinthians 3:18 NASB)

The transformation of your character and the regeneration of your humanity is taking place in you *because of the glory of God in you*! (How else could it take place?) The New International Version adds, "with ever-increasing glory."

Oh friends, please listen closely: We need the Eden Glory of God—the regenerative, life-giving, life-sustaining glory of God—in great measure right now. We need a greater measure of the manifest presence of Jesus in us. And we are *meant* to be filled with it. The glory of God is meant to fill our hearts and souls. We can ask for this supernatural grace, so by all means let's do!

Skill
RECEIVING THE EDEN GLORY OF GOD

Read this prayer through first, and then pray it out loud before you continue reading!

Father, Jesus, Holy Spirit, I receive your Glory into my being. I receive the Glory that fills the oceans, the Glory that sustains the sun. I receive the Glory that raised Christ from the dead! I pray that your Eden Glory would fill my heart, soul, mind, and strength. I am your temple, Lord; come and fill your temple with your Glory! I also pray that your Eden Glory would shield me against all forms of Desolation coming over my life. I renounce every agreement I might have made with Desolation, every agreement large and small. I choose you, God. I renounce the Falling Away, and I choose you. Regardless of how I feel, I choose you, Lord. You are my God and Savior. I pray that your Eden Glory would fill my life—restoring me, renewing me, granting me supernatural endurance and resilience. I also invoke your Eden Glory over my life as a shield, over my household and domain. I invoke your glory, love, and kingdom as my constant strength and shield. In the name of the Lord Jesus Christ, ruler of heaven and earth. Thank you, Lord!

This prayer has become so important to me I find myself invoking the phrase "Your glory, your love, your kingdom" all throughout my day.[‡]

[‡] In the audio version of *Resilient*, I'm able to pray with you, guide you through these prayers in a beautiful, personal way—so you might want to listen to that too!

THE FEAR OF NOT HAVING ENOUGH

The primal fear that sweeps over men and women in survival situations is the fear of not having enough. This reaches to the core of human need. It might be food, water, clothing—whatever "enough" means to each person. This panic has overcome many otherwise steady souls.

When Louis Zamperini's B-24 bomber went down in the Pacific during World War II, only three of the eleven men on board survived. They scrambled onto two small life rafts. Each rubber boat was equipped with a few basic emergency provisions, including military issue Ration D chocolate bars—a single square per man, morning and evening. But during their very first night at sea, while two men slept, the third was overcome by the primal fear of not having enough. He ate every single bar.

> *Louie woke with the sun. Mac was beside him, lying back. Phil lay in his raft, his mind still fumbling. Louie sat up and ran his eyes over the sky and ocean in search of rescuers.*
>
> *Only the sharks stirred. Louie decided to divvy up breakfast, a single square of chocolate. He untied the raft pocket and looked in. All of the chocolate was gone. He looked around the rafts. No chocolate, no wrappers. His gaze paused on Mac. The sergeant looked back at him with wide, guilty eyes.*
>
> *The realization that Mac had eaten all of the chocolate rolled hard over Louie. In the brief time that Louie had known Mac, the tail gunner had struck him as a decent, friendly guy, although a bit of a reveler, confident to the point of flippancy. The crash had undone him.*[1]

Chapter 5

The Assurance of Abundance

A faithful, sensible servant is one to whom the master can give the responsibility of managing his other household servants and feeding them. If the master returns and finds that the servant has done a good job, there will be a reward. I tell you the truth, the master will put that servant in charge of all he owns. But what if the servant is evil and thinks, "My master won't be back for a while," and he begins beating the other servants, partying, and getting drunk?

MATTHEW 24:45–49 NLT

O ne of the funnier and almost iconic videos that came out of the pandemic was a sincere homespun message from a pastor to his congregation. The video was clearly shot on an iPhone at home—because at that point everyone was stuck at home—and the earnest minister was speaking to his flock about overcoming fear. Do not panic; the Lord is in control.

Meanwhile, the shot allowed you to see behind him crates upon crates of toilet paper stockpiled in his living room.

It was painfully self-disclosing, for each and every one of us. The minister was suddenly Everyman, all of us, talking a good game about resilience and all the while scrambling to make sure we had enough.

When the toilet paper stampede hit, I thought it was silly. *Good grief, people, this isn't the Battle of Stalingrad. Chill out.* Then I saw the empty shelves at the market and realized if I didn't join in the grasping, I'd be the guy using grocery bags and banana peels. The hoarding then and the bingeing now are classic symptoms of trauma-survivor behavior. A natural disaster (pandemics are classified as natural disasters) awakens the primal fear that we will not have enough, so we grasp, hoard, stockpile.

I should have invested in toilet paper, hand sanitizer, and cardboard in 2019.

I'm embarrassed to admit how much I've been buying things online ever since the fall of 2020. Packages have been arriving almost daily. When the pandemic first hit, through the spring of the year, I was in rally mode. Stasi and I hunkered down, focused on our life with God, and helped others do the same. But over time my soul kept crying out for comfort, for things to be good again. Unconsciously, I tried to assuage that need through buying stuff. *Millions* of people did. I bought "feel good" things, which for me included fly fishing flies, flannel shirts, camping gear, chocolate, binoculars, and gourmet green tea.

Are we aware, folks, of what we are doing with all this grasping? The fear that overcame Mac in the crash of the B-24 is operating beneath the surface in us, though I didn't really see it for myself until now.

Economic shaking, the fear of death, the loss of normal life, a completely unpredictable future—this sort of catastrophic upheaval drives us all to the core of human need and fear: *Will I be provided for? Will I have enough? Is there abundance for me?*

When you are living in an hour like this one, *any* vulnerability to deprivation and Desolation becomes a high-level vulnerability.

Which leads us to a truly beautiful grace God wants to provide.

What Mother Teaches

The number one word spoken from the lips of wounded and dying soldiers on the battlefield is, "*Mom . . . Mother . . . Ma!*"

Of course it is. From our earliest memories our mother is the source of all comfort, security, nourishment, and help. Mother is mercy. In terms of childhood development, mother comes first, before father.

Starting in the womb, we receive all our nourishment from our mother; we are dependent on her in every way.

Her emotions during pregnancy—especially how she feels about us, about being pregnant—shape our emotions into our adult lives. In the first moments after birth we were placed upon our mother's chest, and our first experience of attachment is with her. We are lifted to her breast, and from her we receive everything we need for our flourishing. As psychologist Robert Karen wrote,

> Emotionally healthy young people, who were both self-reliant and able to rely on others, had had home lives in which both parents were loving and emotionally generous and the mother had given them a feeling of complete security.[2]

On a physical level, the composition of breast milk and what it does for the developing child is simply phenomenal—breast milk enhances brain development, it plays a critical role in the development of the child's immune system, it fortresses the developing baby against a myriad of infections and hospitalizations, and studies have proven it lowers a baby's risk of dying from sudden infant death syndrome (SIDS). On and on the benefits flow; I'm simply naming a few to illustrate how deeply and profoundly *nourishing* a mother was meant to be. Life literally flows from her.[3]

On an emotional level, our fundamental convictions about whether we are going to have enough, if we will be nourished, and blessed—these gut-level, primal convictions come to us through our relationship with our mothers, especially in infancy. Emotional attachment begins during nursing.[4]

The assurance of abundance is something we learn from our mothers—although saying that we learn it sounds way too cerebral, like learning to read. The assurance of abundance—or not—is *imprinted in our souls* and becomes a core conviction.

Before we even learn speech we are forming our deepest beliefs about the world and our place in it through our interactions with our mothers. We learn primal love. We learn primal nourishment. When a child is nursing, it gets to drink its fill, assuring the developing soul of the child, *My needs matter, I will be sated, I will be satisfied, I will have enough.*

Something else is also taking place in these early months and years. The mother is bestowing on her child what I call "the benediction of being." You are celebrated for being here. Your very existence brings joy to the world, and because of that your existence is blessed through nourishment, attention, delight, and attachment-love. This blessedness is something the mother pours forth upon her child without being told to do so. In *Deep Survival*, Laurence Gonzales wrote,

> Psychologists have observed that one of the most basic human needs, beginning at birth, is to be gazed upon by another. Mothers throughout the world have been observed spending long periods staring into the eyes of their babies with a characteristic tilt of the head. To be seen is to be real, and without another to gaze upon us, we are nothing. Part of the terror of being lost [in the wilderness] stems from the idea of never being seen again.[5]

Resilience is bestowed upon us by being adored and by experiencing our deep hunger satisfied with overwhelming abundance. I think it is utterly profound that the infant first receives its immune system from its mother.[6] Physically, emotionally, soulfully, spiritually, God designed that we would receive resilience and immunity through our attachment with our mothers.

That was the original intent, at least.

Mother "Desolation"

Dallas Willard was only two and a half years old when his mother died. It was 1938; his mother and father had gone bankrupt during the Depression and lost their family business just before Dallas was born.[7] They lived a hard rural life. Dallas's mother Maymie suffered an injury jumping from a hay wagon. A subsequent surgery was botched, and she never recovered. Maymie wrote her children poems from the hospital—another beautiful picture of the emotional assurance a mother offers her children—but she would never return home. The loss of his mother was "incomprehensible" to this precious little boy not even three. During the funeral or wake, little Dallas tried to climb into his mother's casket.[8]

In all my years as a therapist I've never heard a more poignant story.

Losing a mother, never having a mother, or living with a mother who in many ways could not offer the mothering we needed is simply devastating. There is no other way to describe it; the research is overwhelming on this point.

Resilience is bestowed

upon us by being adored

and by experiencing our

deep hunger satisfied with

overwhelming abundance.

Psychologist Robert Karen conducted a sweeping review of the research on mother attachment. He reported with devastating precision scores of the early discoveries of mother absence on a child. This story is representative of hundreds like it:

> We are in an unnamed Institution. In grainy, flickering images, we are shown Jane, a little black baby, just after her mother had been forced to leave her for what would turn out to be a three-month period. She's a happy, approachable baby, smiling and giggling as an adult observer plays with her. We are then shown Jane one week later. It is painful to recognize that this is the same child—depressed, eyes searching, completely unresponsive except, finally, for a tremendous, hopeless, frowning wail. [The clinician] cannot soothe the child. She kicks and sobs in terrible agony. . . . [These symptoms] lasted the entire three months her mother was gone. Looking at this child, we feel we are experiencing sadness at its ultimate depth, the most profound grief imaginable.[9]

The kind of grief that makes a little boy climb into his mother's casket.

Karen went on to point out that mother deprivation takes place in many ways that are much less noticeable than total abandonment, yet equally devastating:

> Of course, for many babies, even from their earliest days, mother-love is compromised in fundamental ways. Mother is cold and unresponsive much of the time; mother is

unable to meet the needs of a very demanding or temperamental infant; mother is too preoccupied with herself and her feelings of deprivation to give of herself fully; mother is bitter and angry, and her rage boils over in fits.[10]

I realize I'm taking you into deep, sacred territory. We will proceed gently, because this deprivation is something Jesus desperately wants to heal.

The need is so primal, the role of mother is so truly sacred, it makes naming mother deprivation in our own lives often very difficult. Especially when we had a mother who "did her best." What will help us name our need, the need we are bringing to God, is to ask ourselves,

* Are my reactions to hardship as an adult proving that I received—beyond a shadow of a doubt—the assurance of abundance as a child?
* Are my actions and emotions proving that I received utter assurance that my needs matter, and that they will be met, and met joyfully?

The mother of a friend of mine was a bright, intelligent, attractive woman with loads of energy. She put herself through grad school while he was a young boy, which meant she was gone a great deal of the time. What he came to discover as an adult was that his mother was a very unattached woman herself, and so while she did offer vacations, gourmet meals, and good books, what she did *not* offer was simply herself. She withheld the fundamental attachment and nourishment he craved as a boy. He later wrote me,

A few years ago my wife and I were on holiday in New Zealand. Out in the countryside, you're surrounded by sheep fields. There's sheep everywhere. It was spring, so it was lambing season. I was watching this mother sheep with her lamb; they had been bedded down for a rest when the mother sheep stood up, decided that she's going to cross the meadow and go somewhere else to graze. Her little lamb stood up right with her and, as she took off, he stayed right on her flank. They were practically one.

I'm watching this, and I'm watching my soul watching this, and I realized, *I have absolutely no category for that. I look in that folder and there's nothing there.*

Watching that little lamb, I was thinking, *What if his mother offered him nothing? What if she completely disappeared one day from the field?*, which is what happened to my mom. She went back to work when I was very young and really never came home. All these years I've wondered why I didn't feel particularly attached to my mom. Now I see—it was because she was never attached to me.

You could call this the category of "mother wounds," but I think a far more accurate description is mother *desolation*. The soul is meant to receive profound nourishment from our mother—physically and emotionally, nourishment in absolute abundance. When it doesn't, the soul experiences a famine of the most serious kind.

What lies for you in the folder of your mother, mothering, mother-love?

That might be too big a question. Start with this: Did you receive the assurance of abundance?

In his research Karen discovered a direct link between mother deprivation and juvenile thievery. Children and teenagers we would call "troubled youth," those with compulsive tendencies to steal things, all had histories of mother deprivation:

> Although all stole repeatedly and compulsively, the thefts were often pointless, and two of the boys would destroy any presents given to them. . . . None of them seemed to have any sense of the meaning of what they had done. They could not say why they stole, and they seemed impervious to the wrong done to others. A child who's been separated from his mother . . . not only craves her love but also the symbols of her love. And so, typically, the young thieves stole milk, food, or money to buy food. These are the things they naturally associate with gratification. Often they stole from their mothers . . . a tragically perfect symbolic act.[11]

Perhaps including a perfectly symbolic act like hoarding toilet paper.

Even the best of mothers fail at some point, for we are all broken people in a shipwrecked world. Unmet cravings for security, love, blessing, and nourishment carry on into adulthood. What I want to point out is that any measure of deprivation here, in such a primal need, leaves us vulnerable to Desolation.

And God has provision for us.

Salvation as a New Attachment

A great deal has been written about Dallas Willard since his passing in 2013. The influence of this great man will only grow. But I found the following story to be above and beyond all others the most important. This is especially powerful when you remember the little boy trying to climb into his mother's casket.

> Dallas Willard sat across from me with tears in his eyes as he looked at the floor. Dallas had only weeks to live, but his tears were not for his own life. "What I have learned in this last year," he told me, "is more important than what I learned in the rest of my life. But I have no time to write about it. I will try to finish the projects I have started." He looked up at me. I wondered if he was thinking about our conversation or something else.
>
> "You need to write about this," Dallas said. His voice was steady but with mounting passion: "I know of no soteriology [doctrine of salvation] based on forming a new attachment with God." . . .
>
> The only kind of love that helps the brain learn better character is attachment love. The brain functions that determine our character are most profoundly shaped by who we love. Changing character, as far as the brain is concerned, means attaching in new and better ways.
>
> This realization brought Dallas to tears. If the quality of our human attachments creates human character, is it possible that when God speaks of love, "attachment" is what God means?[12]

The redemption of Dallas's story is so beautiful. The little boy who lost his mother before the age of three, the man who went on to become one of the most brilliant voices for Christianity in the twentieth century, discovered at the end of his life his most important lesson—salvation is a new *attachment*, the soul's loving bond to our loving God.

We've all heard a good bit about our heavenly Father, but in human development mother comes before father, and a new world of love opens to us when we discover that God offers to mother us too—to come and heal our souls here, in this essential place. God yearns to bring us the assurance of abundance: "Can a mother forget the baby at her breast and have no compassion on the child she has borne? Though she may forget, I will not forget you!" (Isaiah 49:15).

God loves you more tenderly and more irrevocably than the best of mothers. If this is new terrain for you, remember—God created motherhood, mothering, mother-love, and the mother-need in each human soul. God is the source of all mothering.

For the soul to be truly saved, for us to come home, our soul needs the loving attachment that mother-love first illustrates for us. Just as we move from our earthly fathers to our homecoming with our true Father, so we need to come home to the mother-love of God, regardless of what we learned from our earthly mothers.

The close of the book of Isaiah crescendos with the promises of the coming kingdom and our Lord's return. The hope described here is exquisitely beautiful; it touches

God loves you more tenderly

and more irrevocably than

the best of mothers.

our longings to find Eden again. Look at how much mother imagery and mother-love fills these final passages:

> For you will nurse and be satisfied
> at . . . comforting breasts;
> you will drink deeply
> and delight in . . . overflowing abundance.
>
> (66:11)

The primal assurance of abundance! It's all there—attachment as through nursing, the comfort we so desperately need, drinking deeply from unlimited resources, healing our souls with the assurance of abundance. God promises to do this for your soul, whatever your mother-story is.

I adore the tenderness promised in the next few lines:

> You will nurse and be carried . . .
> and dandled on her knees.
> As a mother comforts her child,
> so will I comfort you. . . .
> When you see this, your heart will rejoice
> and you will flourish like grass.
>
> (vv. 12–14)

"Dandled on her knees" is such a touching promise. You've seen the best mothers coddle, cuddle, and bounce their little ones on their knees, mother and child thoroughly attached, free to be playful. This is for you! God repeats again the promise of mother-comfort, and the result of all this mothering is the assurance of abundance—our hearts will rejoice, our souls will "flourish like grass"!

Now listen very carefully—you don't need to understand it all, and you don't need to process your entire story with your mother to receive *everything* God is offering here. We heal from the past as we experience new mothering. So let's not wait one moment longer to begin to take hold of this!

Attaching to God

The good news in all attachment research is that attachment deprivations can be healed. Mature adults can go on to form deeply meaningful attachments in their lives.[13]

This is especially true when God steps into the picture:

> God is described over two hundred times in the Old Testament as being *hesed/chesed*, a quality God also desires from us: "For I delight in loyalty [*hesed*] rather than sacrifice" (Hosea 6:6). The Hebrew word *hesed* is translated as "devoted," "faithful," and "unchanging love." Could God be speaking of an attachment love that sticks with us?[14]

We can answer this with a resounding *yes*!

The One who thought of something as beautiful as mother-love, motherhood, and mother-need promises us that "Even if mothers were to forget, I could never forget you!" and "Even if my father and mother abandon me, the LORD will hold me close" (Isaiah 49:15 NET; Psalm 27:10 NLT).

Our need for attachment, mother-love, and the assurance of abundance opens up for us new levels of joyful experience, even in passages that have been familiar to us for years: "I am the vine; you are the branches. If you remain in me and I in you, you will bear much fruit; apart from me you can do nothing" (John 15:5).

You are a "branch." Branches have no unending source of resilience in themselves. They need to draw all of their life and all of their resources from another—they need to *receive* nourishment just as a child does at its mother's breast. God is the fountain of life. The only fountain of life. His glorious life is meant to flow through us every day—healing us, filling us with creativity, courage, joy, playfulness, and resilience. It comes through attachment, bonded love, the soul's union with God.

The goal of Christian faith is so much more than church attendance or holding certain doctrinal beliefs. The destiny of every human soul is *union with God*.[15] As the Scottish Puritan Henry Scougal wrote, "[Christians] know by experience that true religion is a union of the soul with God, a real participation of the divine nature."[16]

Perhaps the trauma of these years will open up for us a startling new understanding, a new hope—loving union with God means *attachment* to God in the very place of mother-need in us.

Dallas's mind raced ahead of mine in our conversations about attachment. He wondered, "Is salvation itself a new and active attachment with God that forms and transforms our identities?" In the human brain, identity and character are formed by who we love. Attachments are powerful and long lasting. Ideas can be changed much more easily. Salvation through a new, loving attachment to God that changes our identities would be a very relational way to understand our salvation. We would be both saved and transformed through attachment love from, to, and with God.[17]

So what do we do?

We attach to God. We ask God for mothering. We go to the place in our souls where mother-need lies; we go to the place of the assurance of abundance, we go to our primal fears, *and we open our hearts to God*. This is so important in times of crisis, suffering, or deprivation.

Skill
RECEIVING ATTACHMENT AND THE
ASSURANCE OF ABUNDANCE

Creator of my soul, Creator of all mother-love and mother-need, I need you here.

I need your mother-love. I need the assurance of abundance. I need the benediction of my being. I need a deep, bonded love with you. I need attachment here, in the place of my soul you created for attachment. Come, healing God, and heal me here in the place of mother. I open my story of mothering to you, God. I invite you into my need for primal love, primal nourishment. Nourish me here, just as you promised.

Creator of my soul, Creator of all mother-love and mother-need, I invite you into my need for primal connection. I invite you into my need for the primal blessing of my being, my existence.

Forgive me for taking this need to other places. I am giving all this to you, God; I am opening it to you now. I forgive my mom. I do. I forgive her and release her, and I invite your mother-love and mother nourishment, your comfort and solace into this place in my soul. Fill me with attachment love; fill me with the assurance of abundance. Come into my primal fears that there will not be enough for me, and fill me with the assurance of abundance. In Jesus' name, amen.

CRISIS EXPOSES WHO WE ARE

The year 1996 was a particularly deadly climbing season on Mount Everest. Severe storms left many climbers in what is called the "death zone" high on the mountain. Three Indian climbers attempting the summit from the northeast ridge were stranded in a devastating blizzard. Unable to descend, they spent the night on the face of the mountain, without shelter of any kind, in a howling storm. The next morning, two Japanese climbers ascending by the same route came upon them; the Indian climbers were near death. But the Japanese offered no assistance of any kind—no food, no water, no bottled oxygen. They didn't even speak to them, but simply stepped to the side and took their rest a few hundred feet beyond. After they made the summit, on their descent, they left the Indians to die as they passed them by.[1]

Chapter 6

Unconverted Places

Now Peter was sitting out in the courtyard, and a servant girl came to him. "You also were with Jesus of Galilee," she said. But he denied it before them all. "I don't know what you're talking about," he said. Then he went out to the gateway, where another servant girl saw him and said to the people there, "This fellow was with Jesus of Nazareth." He denied it again, with an oath: "I don't know the man!" After a little while, those standing there went up to Peter and said, "Surely you are one of them; your accent gives you away." Then he began to call down curses, and he swore to them, "I don't know the man!" Immediately a rooster crowed.
MATTHEW 26:69–74

S urvival situations bring out the best and the worst in
people.

Who we are, what we love, and how far we are willing to trust God are revealed when we are truly hard pressed.

There is poor Peter, of course, and the call of the rooster. But another revealing story—especially in terms of the fear of not having enough—comes to us from the life of the young church. Things are still turbulent. Revival is happening, but so is persecution. The infamous Ananias and Sapphira sell some real estate, and the problem isn't that they kept part of the cash for themselves; the issue is they *pretend* they are sharing it all with the poor. They want to look sacrificial while living selfishly. The duplicity is the issue. I think the fear of not having enough causes them to hoard, but they lie to the apostles and say they aren't. Things don't go so well after that.

Pressure brings it all to the surface.

Military training is designed to do exactly this—strip away all pretense and expose what's really in you, see what you're made of. All those popular outdoor leadership programs have a similar goal but take a less severe approach. They simply drop people into the backcountry—far beyond the Comfort Culture—push them past their normal limits, and see what comes out.

Most of the time what comes out is not something we wanted the world to see.*

I enjoy watching those wilderness survival reality shows not only because I adore the wilderness but because as a therapist I love the raw look into the inner world of hard-pressed

---

* Marriage and parenting do this too, famously so, but it takes place over years not weeks, and less publicly, so the exposure isn't as immediate. But you are revealed for who you are nevertheless. How you respond to these challenges is one of your most important tests.

human beings. Everybody knows how to put on a brave face; what I want to see is what's beneath. If you've ever watched any of those shows you've seen it—how their biggest battle ends up not being cold or hunger but their inner demons.

I'm bringing this up because we are trying to thoroughly strengthen our souls' "immune systems" for trying times. There are pockets of resistance in us that will prove our downfall if we don't bring them to Christ.

The Sweet Safety of Holiness

Now may the God of peace make you holy in every way, and may your whole spirit and soul and body be kept blameless until our Lord Jesus Christ comes again. (1 Thessalonians 5:23 NLT)

I absolutely love this verse; I love the hope of my entire being made pure by the Spirit of God.

I realize that *holiness* is a word with a lot of baggage for many people, but we can get past all that if we look at the gorgeous life and character of Jesus—he was simply good through and through. His character is so alluring, so winsome, and whenever you see him relating to people you are watching true holiness in action. Women who everyone had used and abused came to Jesus, threw themselves at his feet, and he was only loving toward them. Sometimes the crowds loved him, other times they shouted for his head, but he didn't let it faze him. Jesus' goodness in the Gospels is captivating.

When his own time of severe testing came, that goodness

was his shield. Just before the secret police came for him, before the grisly scenes that follow, Jesus told his disciples, "I will no longer talk much with you, for the ruler of this world is coming, and he has nothing in Me" (John 14:30 NKJV).

The enemy tried every angle he could find on Jesus—seduction, rejection, threat, the fear of not having enough, even torture. Nothing worked, because Satan had nothing "in" Jesus to use as his hook. Imagine the sheer relief of it.

It probably feels like obtaining even a fraction of that goodness is beyond you, but the promise of the Christian faith is that God *will* reproduce Jesus' goodness in you: "I feel as if I'm going through labor pains for you again, and they will continue until Christ is fully developed in your lives" (Galatians 4:19 NLT).

The goal of God's work in us is Jesus taking up residence in every part of us. Nothing left out. No little pockets of resistance. (And did you notice? Paul, with the Holy Spirit through him, is "mothering" these dear followers of Christ toward the beautiful goal. He is "in labor" with them, for them!)

In our own times of severe testing, we want to be made "holy in every way," our entire "spirit and soul and body . . . kept blameless" (1 Thessalonians 5:23 NLT). Let me be quick to add, I think much of the testing and the Falling Away takes place very subtly in the heart. It's the small turns from God toward our other comforters, the quiet feelings of being disappointed with him, the early stages of Desolation—this is how most of the testing plays out. But it has momentum like an avalanche.

C. S. Lewis's personal secretary was a man named Walter Hooper. He described the Oxford professor and creator of Narnia as "the most thoroughly converted man I ever met."[2] What a wonderful thing to be said about you. Lewis was a man whose entire being—heart, soul, mind, and strength—had become almost thoroughly inhabited by Jesus Christ. His fragmented self was nearly fully reintegrated in Christ. (Nearly, because none of us are utterly whole until Christ returns. But my goodness—*nearly* is fabulous.) Many people fell in love with the presence of Dallas Willard for the same reason.

Let me pause on that thought for a moment, because while this is known to the saints, the Comfort Culture framed within us other goals. Does your heart tell you that it agrees with this—that the goal of your life is to become the most converted person your friends and family know?

Or does your heart prefer the goal to be something else? Perhaps, "I just want things to be good again, and let somebody else live through the end of the age"? Ouch. That hits close to home.

The battle taking place over the human heart can be described as Satan using every form of seduction and threat to take our hearts captive and our loving Jesus doing everything he can to form single-heartedness in us. This often plays out in thousands of small, daily choices. Which is kind, really; we want to develop single-heartedness *before* the severe testing comes.

Theodore Roosevelt had a lifetime of stories to prepare him for his last great adventure and ordeal—descending an unnavigated tributary of the Amazon in primitive canoes. And he needed preparation, because he nearly died on that trip. But this is the fellow who rode eighteen hours

The battle taking place over the human heart can be described as Satan using every form of seduction and threat to take our hearts captive and our loving Jesus doing everything he can to form single-heartedness in us.

on horseback across the Dakota Badlands without water because the spring from which they'd planned to get water had dried up.

I love another story about a hunting trip during which Roosevelt and his guide repeatedly got their wagon stuck in mud as they tried to travel into the mountains.

> The second plunge of the horses brought them up to their bellies in the morass, where they stuck. It was freezing cold, with the bitter wind blowing, and the bog holes were skimmed with ice; so that we passed a thoroughly wretched two hours while freeing the horses and unloading the wagon. . . . My companion preserving an absolutely unruffled temper throughout . . . whistling the "Arkansas Traveller." At one period, when we were up to our waists in the icy mud, it began to sleet and hail, and I muttered that I would "rather it didn't storm"; whereat he stopped whistling for a moment to make the laconic rejoinder, "We're not having our rathers this trip."[3]

A whole lot of that gets you ready for just about anything. Maybe this helps you reinterpret the story of your own life. Maybe all those former hardships were developing resilience in you!

Love Over Hatred

As Jesus began to explain the trials of the final hours, he warned us several times about hatred, and how hanging on to love will prove very difficult: "And many will turn away from me and betray and hate each other. . . . Sin will be rampant everywhere, and the love of many will grow cold" (Matthew 24:10, 12 NLT).

Wow. If this doesn't describe our times, I don't know what does. You can't express one single opinion online without receiving poisonous retaliation. Humanity is raw and angry (there's the trauma at work). Hatred is ruining all public discourse. I know of many churches whose beautiful congregations have been completely fractured over the issue of in-person gatherings or no, over masks or no, over vaccines or no. Church attendance has fallen to less than 50 percent of pre-COVID numbers, and many churches are barely keeping the lights on. Love grown cold.

Following the global trauma of 2020, I noticed something emerging in the traffic of our neighborhood. Two distinct drivers began to appear. There were the timid drivers, who would stop for eternal periods at intersections before proceeding. Even though they had the right of way, they would hesitate, then ever-so-cautiously move again, as if some terrible accident was about to come upon them. The fear that began with fear of sickness had permeated into a low-level anxiety throughout the rest of their lives.

Then there were the ragers, the folks who would fly up behind me (because they were going twenty miles per hour over the speed limit) and ride my bumper as if they wanted to drive right through me until they had a chance to pass. Both fear and rage are part of the trauma response, and there's lots of it out there now.

I am among them, though my rage behind the wheel

looks far more self-righteous. I *hate* it when the ragers ride someone dangerously close, then pass them in a place they should never try passing. If I'm the guy they are bearing down upon I will slow down even more, forcing them back under the speed limit. But the hatred in my heart is still hatred just the same.

We are hard-pressed, folks, and we aren't exactly shining.

It is our inner weaknesses, brokenness, and frankly the "unconverted places" that are going to take our legs out from under us. As we discussed with the topic of mother desolation, if we have a vulnerability already leaning toward disillusionment, abandonment, and other desolate feelings, this is where Desolation will attack. So we pursue that beautiful attachment to God and the assurance of abundance in order to fortify ourselves against Desolation.

God wants to do this for your entire being. We will not be safe until we are completely his.

Maturity is no longer optional, dear ones; wholeheartedness is no longer something we can go without. Those vulnerabilities in us prove treacherous in this world, like a faulty bridge or a bow that is not properly strung.

Dealing with Our Vulnerabilities

"I don't know that I could live through that." Dozens of people have confessed this to me when we've spoken about the possibility that we are living through the end of the age.

Remember now—there is no zombie apocalypse. You've already lived through trying times. You already know quite a bit about what it means to be hard-pressed; what most people *don't* know is what to do with everything that has surfaced.

A man I counseled years ago, a Christian leader of deep integrity, wrote to me recently. He said, "I don't understand what's happening. I've never really entertained the possibility of an affair until now. But over the course of the last six months, I find myself battling that temptation and feeling like I'm losing the battle. I haven't surrendered but I don't understand what's going on in my heart."

The longing for things to be good again is making us vulnerable to all sorts of compromises. I can help you with this.

First, let's remove the shock and shame of those moments when hard-pressed you suddenly rages, binges, goes faithless, or simply shows up as a very unappealing version of you.

Salvation is a process, not an event.

Oh yes—salvation is a *homecoming* to be sure. That is the event. Our salvation begins when we first turn toward Jesus with an open heart. We come to him for mercy. We ask him to forgive us for living so much of our life utterly ignoring him. We invite him in as our rescuer. We also surrender; we yield the throne of our lives to him. That's the homecoming, and our Father is so absolutely giddy over it he wants to throw you a party. (In fact, the angels *did* party over your homecoming—see Luke 15.)

Our homecoming is utterly life-changing.

But what surprises us, what can really dishearten us, is that it's not *instantaneously* life-changing. Not thoroughly, that is. This is because salvation is also the re-creation of

Salvation is a process,

not an event.

our fallen humanity, a restoration of our life through union with Christ. And that happens over time.

> The way of the righteous is like the first gleam of dawn, which shines ever brighter until the full light of day. (Proverbs 4:18 NLT)

> For by one sacrifice he has made perfect forever those who are being made holy. (Hebrews 10:14)

Note the process clearly laid out in these verses—dawn to day, cleansed and now being made holy.

But you already know this to be true; you're living out the process every day.

Parts of you seem well-inhabited by Christ. The rest of you seems practically pagan (revealed in your driving, bingeing, media choices, fantasy life, or the desire for life to be good again overwhelming all other faculties). How can these parts exist in the same human being? Because we are like stained glass—beautiful even in our brokenness, but made up of many fragments.

Everyone is fragmented.

Part of me loves God, confessed the apostle Paul, *and part of me rebels* (see Romans 7). This condition is why David cried out, "Give me an undivided heart!" (Psalm 86:11). This is why salvation is a *process*, and it will help you be kind and merciful when those unconverted parts of you suddenly show up. Simply because the rage, bitterness, unbelief, or whatever pops out of the closet doesn't mean your salvation isn't real. It means parts of you are yet to be united to Christ. So let's talk about how to get them united with Jesus, because we are in dire need of the resilience that holiness provides.

The Salvation That Is Truly Salvation

Jesus also used this illustration: "The Kingdom of Heaven is like the yeast a woman used in making bread. Even though she put only a little yeast in three measures of flour, it permeated every part of the dough" (Matthew 13:33 NLT).

Yeast gets into the dough and slowly works its way through the entire batch. The promise is this: the goodness of Jesus *will* work its way through your entire being. Jesus is the yeast, by the way—it is his gorgeous life living in you that begins to permeate your being and truly save you. That is what salvation is: the permutation of your being by the presence of Christ in you, healing you, renewing you, imbuing you with his own life. Nineteenth-century Scottish author and minister George MacDonald wrote,

> The notion that the salvation of Jesus is a salvation from the consequences of our sins, is a false, mean, low notion. The salvation of Christ is salvation from the smallest tendency or leaning to sin. It is a deliverance into the pure air of God's ways of thinking and feeling. It is a salvation that makes the heart pure, with the will and choice of the heart to be pure.[4]

It follows, then, that what we are cooperating with, what we seek with all our hearts in this hard hour, is the process where God exposes some part of us *not yet* united to Christ, so that it *can* be united to Christ. This is the new way of looking at the stuff that emerges when you are hard-pressed.

This is why the military and those outdoor leadership programs have such good results—they provide for live, in-the-moment experiences of dealing with your stuff. But so does Christianity, and you don't even have to leave town.

Skill
CONVERTING THE "UNCONVERTED PLACES"

Oh Jesus, I pray for the salvation that is truly salvation.

This is what I have found myself praying. I've been a Christian for almost five decades. I know I am secure in God's love. I know I am forgiven. But I cringe when these unconverted places surface in me. I don't merely want to be forgiven; I want to be truly saved, meaning *permeated by Christ.*

This is how it typically happens: the bitterness or lust or whatever has just shown up, and in that moment I pray for the salvation that is truly salvation and I ask that this part of me is utterly converted too. Let's take it step-by-step from there.

Don't run. Don't hide. You've been exposed. The instinctual response is to put a fig leaf over it. That won't help. Stay with the exposure—you need Christ right here.

Enter the unconverted place. By this I mean you *go there*, feel it, open it to the light of day. This is a part of you, so walk right into the middle of it. You want to open the door of this fragment to Christ, and the door opens from the inside.

Okay Jesus—here I am—hateful, lustful, resentful. I see it; I feel it. Now I open this part of me to you, Lord. Save me here.

Asking for Jesus to "save you here" is far more than, "I'm sorry" (though "I'm sorry" might be needed). You are not merely apologizing and promising to do better; that doesn't work. *You are seeking for this place to be united with Jesus Christ*, and therefore in his care, able to receive re-creation.[†]

Oh Jesus, save me here. I surrender this unconverted place in me to you, to your indwelling presence. Unite with me here; permeate me here. I pray to be completely converted here.

Then pause. Ask Jesus what is needed. Is there angry defiance that needs to be released? Does something need to be surrendered here—your need to be right or get even, your self-comforters (meaning your addictions)?

Jesus, what else is needed? Show me how to cooperate with you.

Jesus, unite with every part of me that is not yet united with you. Integrate my entire being into one, whole person united with you. I pray for complete union with you throughout my being. For you alone are my salvation, and I ask you for the salvation that is truly salvation right here. I ask for your holiness here. In your name.

Now let me add something that will help your heart back toward joy.

Our enemy is filled with hate and is sending hatred into the

---

† I am not suggesting the existence of unsanctified places in us means we have lost the security of our homecoming to God. Not at all. But salvation is also a re-creation, and in this sense we are not yet his here.

world—especially against the saints. No doubt you've felt this come upon you, though perhaps you didn't name it as a spiritual attack. It comes as contempt, diminishment, accusation. It comes as a sense of failure, and especially the loss of the wonderful knowledge of God's love for you. When this has demonic power behind it, when it comes from a *spirit* of hatred, it pierces heart and soul.

It also tempts you to hate, fills you with feelings of hatred toward someone or something else.

You can't talk yourself out of this kind of attack. Spiritual piercing requires heavenly power to cut off. And there is no greater power in the universe than the love of God. "For you bless the godly, O LORD; you surround them with your shield of love" (Psalm 5:12 NLT).

Our ministry team has found it very effective to actually *enforce* the love of God through prayer against all hatred.

I renounce all hatred. I renounce every agreement I've been making with hatred in any form. I renounce all cooperation or participation with hatred. I also renounce all hatred coming against me; I reject it from my life. My Father loves me. The Lord Jesus loves me. I choose the way of love. I choose love! So now I proclaim and enforce the mighty love of God against all hatred coming against me, in the name of Jesus Christ. I pray the shield of your love, Father, to protect my heart and soul from every attack of hatred. In Jesus' name, amen.

MIRAGES AND ILLUSIONS

Mirages have always been a dilemma for the survivor, especially as time drags on and the desire to find refuge grows intense. Our longing for something to be true overwhelms our reason and senses in order to conjure it into reality. Steven Rinella, hunting above the Arctic Circle, was consumed more than once by the vast terrain of the Arctic and its puzzling light.

> *There was a very strong atmospheric refraction in that direction; the seam between the land and the air shimmered and danced crazily, like an exaggerated version of heat waves coming off a highway in the desert. . . .*
>
> *The Canadian-born explorer Vilhjalmur Stefansson, who passed through this same country just about a hundred years before me, talked a lot about the trickiness of Arctic light. He once mistook an up-close ground squirrel for a faraway grizzly. He tells of another hunter who mistook a three- or four-ounce lemming for a musk ox weighing several hundred pounds. He also mentions a man who steered his boat toward a "dark mountain with glacier-filled valleys on either side." It was actually a walrus's head, and the glaciers were its tusks.[1]*

Sometimes the illusions become dangerous. Climber Aron Ralston was trapped in a slot canyon for days when a massive boulder shifted and pinned his arm. Desperate for escape, he thought the sounds of crow calls were the cries of people looking for him.

Chapter 7

The Kingdom Without the King

Watch out that no one deceives you. For many will come in my name, claiming, "I am the Messiah," and will deceive many.

MATTHEW 24:4–5

I n the little town of Kapaa, Kauai, there's a museum dedicated to an "Eden experiment" that took place in the 1960s on the gorgeous North Shore. It was called Taylor Camp because the brother of the famous actress Elizabeth Taylor was a founder of this community of hippies, surfers, and Vietnam vets who fled the campus riots and police brutality on the mainland to live together . . . naked . . . in tree houses.

It was "the ultimate hippie fantasy."[2] And honestly—it sounds pretty wonderful at first.

Living for free without a care in the world in paradise—no nine-to-five, no mortgage, no bills, no worries. You don't need to work at all, just live off the land—the mangoes, avocados, and other fruits are falling from the trees. Lie around in the lush beauty and warmth of the tropics, play music, get high, have sex, romp in the ocean. What's a little drug abuse and immorality among friends?

But we know now that the 1960s had a dark underbelly. The drug abuse and sexual foraging were deeply damaging. AIDS was just one of the fruits. "Make Love Not War," sounded good, but a lot of women and men were hurt following that siren song. My buddy Craig tried the hippie life real hard, hitchhiking all over the United States, Central America, and Europe, doing drugs and "dropping out," as the saying goes. Most of his friends died of overdose; some are still in mental institutions. He said, "I barely escaped."

Maybe Jesus had this heartache in mind when he repeatedly warned us about rampant deception toward the end of the age—false saviors, false expressions of the kingdom of God, counterfeit Edens.

"Many will come," meaning there's going to be lots of it. "And will deceive many," meaning lots of folks are going to fall for it. Jesus seemed genuinely concerned, as if the deceptions are going to be very convincing. He began the Olivet Discourse here, and then he repeated his warning at the close:

> Then if anyone tells you, "Look, here is the Messiah,"
> or "There he is," don't believe it. For false messiahs and

false prophets will rise up and perform great signs and wonders so as to deceive, if possible, even God's chosen ones. See, I have warned you about this ahead of time. (Matthew 24:23–25 NLT)

A good teacher repeats things when he wants to make especially sure we don't forget.

I don't think this is limited to some crackpot claiming to be the Messiah. Jesus understands both our intense longing for life to be good again and the proven abilities of our enemy to lure us into false relief—which inevitably fails, making us vulnerable to a loss of heart and of faith. This will play out on a cultural level, but the vast majority will take place in the quiet movements of the human heart.

I'm grateful Jesus assured us that God's chosen ones will be able to escape this, but the way he said it, you get the feeling he meant *barely*.

We are especially vulnerable to counterfeit Edens in this hour. Our longing for relief is trying hard to overrule all other values. Just this morning I walked past one of Stasi's garden-and-home magazines lying open to a photo that could almost have been a form of pornography. But the seduction was Eden. The photo looked out the open French doors of a luxury home, across the gorgeous pool and patio to the rolling green hills of a beautiful estate.

My heart took one look and said, *That's it. That's all I need now to be happy.*

That's how fast the deceit and the seduction happen.

The Backlash of False Saviors

While they were listening to this, he went on to tell them a parable, because he was near Jerusalem and the people thought that the kingdom of God was going to appear at once. He said: "A man of noble birth went to a distant country to have himself appointed king and then to return. So he called ten of his servants and gave them ten minas. "Put this money to work," he said, "until I come back." But his subjects hated him and sent a delegation after him to say, "We don't want this man to be our king." (Luke 19:11–14)

In his famous song "Imagine," John Lennon offered a vision of a world made new. Millions of people loved that song. It sounded so beautiful—we can make a world of peace and brotherhood: no possessions, no war, no hatred. Flower power. It was so alluring. Many thought it was the realization of their heart's deepest desires. But it was a colossal disaster. Lennon tapped into a childlike kingdom longing, fueled by adolescent rebellion. Notice that Lennon wanted no heaven, no hell, no religion. There's no place for God in Lennon's Eden. (It's important to pay attention to *everything* a false prophet is saying.) He wanted the kingdom without the King.

This runs *deep* in human nature. It was sown in us by the evil one himself, back at the fall of mankind when we chose life over God, and it is utterly and thoroughly demonic.

The 1960s seem pretty innocent compared to most historic attempts to usher in the kingdom without the King. Every single one of those efforts to create heaven on earth became a living hell.

During the Russian Revolution, the Bolsheviks promised to end war, give land to the peasants, bread to urban workers—it sounded like the common man was finally going to get equal rights. What *actually* happened is that ten million people were killed and a ruthless, oppressive regime was established, the legacy of which 287 million people stagger under today.

Or take the Great Leap Forward in China—it sounded so enlightened. The Rolling Stones, Sartre, John Lennon, and the early leaders of the feminist movement all embraced Chairman Mao because they thought he would fight for the working class and bring about a more just world order. Instead forty to eighty million people died and another ruthless regime was created.[3] And let's not forget that Hitler's Germany was a vision of an ideal world. Not only did they exterminate Jews but they also tried to rid their ideal society of the handicapped and disabled.

I'm using historical examples because at this point they have few defenders, although only a few years ago these movements were the darling of the intellectual elite. If I use contemporary examples I'm going to start a fistfight because folks *do not like it* when you question their Eden agendas.

The governments of this world are growing dangerously oppressive. We can no longer agree as a society on what is good and evil. There's no consensus on what human beings were made to be, how we should live. So the fight for justice has collapsed into heavy-handed policies for every human being to live any way they want, no matter how far from what God created us to be. If you attempt to stand against these movements, you will be crucified with a sort of self-righteous vengeance that has the tones of religious persecution.

I'm only bringing this up because Jesus warned us about it.

Tired souls are willing to go along with just about anything, so long as we are promised we can have our own little happiness back. When I was visiting a friend in eastern Europe a few years ago, he said many people were willing to go back to communism because at least it meant security! "To a ravenous appetite even the bitter is sweet" (Proverbs 27:7 NRSV).

Jesus said, "The poor you will always have with you" (Matthew 26:11). He was not being cynical. He was being realistic. Everything Jesus said was grounded in open-eyed realism. The Scriptures are clear: the world will never be made right again apart from the return of Jesus Christ. Do we really believe this?

Of course we do what we can to make the world a better place. But we run from any and every attempt to make the world a *perfect* place—that's Hitler's Germany, Mao's China, even Taylor Camp.

We've got to remember, folks, that no matter how promising an idea sounds, if God's not in it, you don't want to be in it either. This is true of a relationship, career change, buying or selling a house, even something as simple as a vacation. We only want what Jesus is in; we only want what our Father is giving. The key test for *this* moment is not only "I give you my allegiance, Jesus" but also "I only want what you are doing."

And what is Jesus doing right now?

No matter how promising an
idea sounds, if God's not in it,
you don't want to be in it either.

Is he trying to secure a happy little life for everyone on the planet?

Or is he trying to prepare every human heart and soul for his sudden, surprising return? Only the return of Jesus will bring about the healing of this broken planet.

Bodyguarding Your Eden Heart

When Jesus says things like, "Don't be alarmed," "Don't let your heart be troubled," and "See that your hearts are not weighed down," he's making an assumption that *we* play an active role in protecting our own hearts. It is we who choose not to allow our hearts to be overtaken by fear or sorrow. It is certainly in our power to choose what we give our hearts over to. The rich experience of having God come for us, speak to us, and move on our behalf can lead us to believe that it's all up to him. But this is not the case.

Remember how I said in chapter 1 that at some point the weary human heart simply comes to the end of its reserves and says, *I'm done now. I don't want to do this anymore*? Well, millions of people started quitting their jobs in 2021, all at the same time, in numbers never before seen. It's called—I kid you not—the Great Resignation.[4]

It could be that a whole lot of people are simply saying, "All this upheaval convinced me that now's the time to go live the life I've always wanted to live." Could be. Might just be a jillion people all deciding to chase their dreams *at the exact same moment*. But it sure looks like the thing we've been talking about in this book—the trauma response, the weary heart, and the grasp for things to be good again. With a 1960s sort of naivete, millions of people are simply walking away from work without a new job in sight.

I fear that the Great Resignation is going to live up to its name. The perfect life isn't out there, friends. The world hasn't suddenly become a magic place again. It's the same disappointing world it's always been. This mass exodus from the workforce feels like a search for Taylor Camp. But disillusionment will soon follow, and you know who's coming after that.

By the way, Taylor Camp didn't enjoy its groove very long. The hippies there had a number of confrontations with the police and locals who didn't like the entire vibe of the thing. It came to a violent end when it was burned to the ground.

Jesus understands Taylor Camp and every effort like it; he really does. He knows everyone has an Eden heart. It's where we come from, our true home. It's what every human being is trying to recover . . . with or without the King. How many affairs have taken place in this hour? Therapist friends who work with men in sexual recovery tell me that pornography use skyrocketed in 2020. Of course it did. Sex is *the* great false Eden. But there are many others—food, alcohol, and buying stuff among them.

The great and terrible Falling Away—that human landslide of weary and bitter hearts—is filled with people who have reached the point where their hearts have simply decided to settle for relief without the King. *I'll take some happiness now, thank you very much, and whatever to the King.* It's that subtle, and that awful. We could call it the

Great Spiritual Resignation. The landslide is seen in the rising number of Christians, many young people included, who are either walking away from God or exchanging their Christianity for a more universalist faith.

Christianity has been linked with so many intolerant movements and partisan politics that many believers are wanting to distance themselves from it and embrace something more inclusive. "God can be found in any faith or no faith at all." I understand the appeal; I truly do. Jesus *is* for everyone:

> Jesus stood and shouted to the crowds, "Anyone who is thirsty may come to me! Anyone who believes in me may come and drink! For the Scriptures declare, 'Rivers of living water will flow from his heart.'" (John 7:37–38 NLT)

> Come to me, all of you who are weary and carry heavy burdens. (Matthew 11:28 NLT)

Jesus' arms could not have been more fully open when he died upon the cross.

But we must not allow ourselves to be swept away by the landslide of all this "tapping out"; in this hour of disappointed hearts, we need to hold fast to the "faith once delivered" (Jude v. 3 YLT). Buddha did not go to the cross for you. Neither did any of the thirty-three million Hindu gods. Mother Earth cannot raise you from the grave. This precious earth waits to be resurrected by its Creator. Before more dear hearts embrace the resignation, we need to clearly say that Christianity, as given to us by Jesus, is not universalism:

Jesus told him, "I am the way, the truth, and the life. No one can come to the Father except through me." (John 14:6 NLT)

There is salvation in no one else! God has given no other name under heaven by which we must be saved. (Acts 4:12 NLT)

As we seek to convert our unconverted places and take hold of the strength that prevails, we need to bodyguard our faith and our Eden hearts back to Jesus. We turn from all other comforters—even benign things like remodeling projects and vacations—to give our hearts fully to Christ.

Where are we chasing life? We must make sure that this tender part of our heart belongs to Jesus.

I love summer. It's Stasi's and my favorite time of year. But here in Colorado we're now deep in the transition to fall, and all of our beautiful flower baskets are going to die. We made our front porch a little Eden refuge this year, a lush botanical garden, and I feel the clock ticking. Something in me rises up in a desperate, *No!* I'm out there every day pruning, feeding, coaxing them along. (There was a freeze predicted last night, so all those flowers are currently in my living room.) I can feel the desperation in my body as I write this. *Please, not yet. Not yet. Don't die yet. I need you for as long as I can have flowers.*

My longing for things to be good again is at an all-time high, so I'm bringing all our flowers into the house like beloved pets, desperate for them to stay lovely just a little longer. Jesus in all his kindness comes along with such

As we seek to convert our

unconverted places and

take hold of the strength

that prevails, we need to

bodyguard our faith and our

Eden hearts back to Jesus.

loving reassurance and says, *You don't need to do that, John. Everything is coming back to you. There's no need to grasp.*

Yes, God our Father—our generous Father—will provide us with the "hors d'oeuvres of Eden" even in times of intense madness. "You prepare a feast for me in the presence of my enemies" (Psalm 23:5 NLT). If we can recognize these moments as gifts to sustain our hearts—if we can hold them with an open hand—they can support us, even bring healing.

The trick is to not make them the focus of our life.

Eden Is a Breath Away

We'd better pause at this point to remind ourselves where we have placed our hope, the hope that is the crown jewel of the Christian faith. We have a hope that is "an anchor for the soul, firm and secure" (Hebrews 6:19), a resilient hope, a hope that *produces* resilience. "We who have run for our very lives to God have every reason to grab the promised hope with both hands and never let go. It's an unbreakable spiritual lifeline, reaching past all appearances right to the very presence of God" (vv. 18–19 THE MESSAGE).

You think I'm talking about heaven; I'm not. Not the typical Christian understanding of heaven—not unless we understand that heaven is the return of Eden.

Jesus Christ gave his life to give each of us a hope above and beyond all former hopes. Every action and teaching of his brilliant life were very intentionally directed at unveiling this hope to us. Late in the gospel of Matthew he described it with breathtaking clarity:

"Truly I tell you, at the renewal of all things, when the Son of Man sits on his glorious throne . . . everyone who has left houses or brothers or sisters or father or mother or wife or children or fields for my sake will receive a hundred times as much and will inherit eternal life. . . ." (Matthew 19:28-29)

The re-creation of the world. When the world is made new. A promise so breathtaking, so shocking and heartbreakingly beautiful I'm stunned that so many have missed it. Oh yes, we've heard quite a bit about "heaven." But Jesus is clearly not talking about heaven here—he is talking about the re-creation of *all things*, including the earth we love. . . .

We have been looking for the Renewal all our lives. It has been calling to us through every precious memory and every moment of beauty and goodness. It is the Promise whispered in every sunrise. Every flower. Every wonderful day of vacation; every pregnancy; the recovery of your health. . . .

If we will listen with kindness and compassion to our own souls, we will hear the echoes of a hope so precious we can barely put words to it, a wild hope we can hardly bear to embrace. God put it there. He also breathed the corresponding Promise into the earth; it is the whisper that keeps coming to us in moments of golden good-ness. But of course. "He has made everything beautiful for its own time. He has planted eternity in the human heart . . ." (Ecclesiastes 3:11 NLT). The secret to your unhappiness and the answer to the agony of the earth are one and the same—we are longing for the kingdom of God. We are aching for the restoration of all things.

That is the only hope strong enough, brilliant enough, glorious enough to overcome the heartache of this world.[5]

Gang, your every wish is about to come true. Your longings are about to be completely and wonderfully fulfilled. *We get Eden back.* The return of Jesus ushers in the restoration of all things, right here on this planet. When John saw the New Jerusalem coming down out of heaven, it was coming to earth!

> I saw the Holy City, the new Jerusalem, coming down out of heaven from God, prepared as a bride beautifully dressed for her husband. And I heard a loud voice from the throne saying, "Look! God's dwelling place is now among the people, and he will dwell with them. They will be his people, and God himself will be with them and be their God. 'He will wipe every tear from their eyes. There will be no more death' or mourning or crying or pain, for the old order of things has passed away." He who was seated on the throne said, "I am making everything new!" (Revelation 21:2–5)

The survivor understands that their present situation is something that they are moving *through*, passing *through*. They are enduring with resilience, which is why Jesus encourages endurance. *This is not my lasting reality; this is simply my present reality*. We are tapping into the help of God and the strength that prevails simply to see us *through* these times. But dear friends, we are heading toward a wonderful, breathtaking turn of events! All of this, all that we are suffering is passing away. Soon we'll be laughing, feasting, and telling the stories. Drinking in all the pleasures of Eden. Forever.

This frame of mind changes everything.

If you tell a survivor that rescue is coming in three weeks, or even three months, they can hang on. They find new strength. They'll make it.

But if you tell that same survivor the hope for rescue will probably not happen until after they die, they will lose all hope. They are left to hunker down and grasp for whatever little crumbs of life they can find.

The Great Rescue is at hand.

This world cannot be healed or set right without the return of its King. We are aching and groaning for Eden restored, and that is exactly what the return of Christ means. Now add to this the reality that we are living in the final moments before his return, right on the precipice of it. These anchors will enable you not to take your Eden heart to any counterfeit, great or small, and will give you a hope so strong you can endure anything.

Skill

GIVING YOUR EDEN HEART TO
JESUS "IN THE MOMENT"

Every time your Eden longings rise up in you, give them to Jesus. There is no other safe place.

When I feel the desperation rising, when I find myself despairing or angry because my plans for Eden are being thwarted, I stop and gently shepherd my heart back into Jesus. It's best to do this in the moment, as you are feeling the intense desire, or as you are being tempted to give your heart to something else. As Carl Jung is reported to have said, "Every addiction is a misplaced prayer."

When we were talking about unconverted places in the previous chapter, I explained how important it is to enter those places in order to open the door to Christ there. This is all the more beautiful to do with our Eden longings. Enter your primal longing for things to be good again, and in that place start loving God. Love him in the longing, and turn to him, saying, "I choose you. I choose you, God. You are my life." I don't dismiss the longing. I don't shame it. I don't try to make it small again. It's there. I feel it. But instead of painting the room or chasing the next dinner or whatever, I enter the primal longing and give it to God.

O Lord Jesus, I give my Eden heart to you and you alone.

I'm so filled with longing, Lord, for things to be good again. I just want . . . [fill in the blank, dear ones—what is it that you want?] I just want things to be beautiful. I just want people to love one another. I want this turmoil to be over. I want evil to stop.

Jesus, catch my Eden heart. I put my hope in the restoration of Eden when you return. I give my heart to you and your return. You are the only safe place. There is only one Eden. I give my heart to the true and only Eden, which you will restore when you return.

This is perhaps the most beautiful thing a human soul ever does. Over and over again, in the thousand little choices, we turn our faces back to God.

I had such a sweet moment the other night as I lingered on the front porch, too spun up to go to bed. I began to say, "I choose you. I love you. Right here in my longing for things to be good again, I choose you. I'm not going to plan a trip right now. I'm not going to go drink a bottle of wine. I'm going to take all that desire and choose you, God." Suddenly the breeze that had been completely still all evening gently caressed my face. Such a tender moment of Jesus replying, *Good choice, John. Well done.*

DIGGING DEEP

Colter Barnes was dropped into the Canadian wilderness in a survival situation just before winter was about to descend. He had with him only his clothes and a handful of survival tools, including a fire starter and fishing line. He successfully built a shelter and was able to start and maintain a fire. But a big man like Colter cannot live on the mushrooms and wild onions he was foraging. It was not enough even to maintain his body weight. He needed fish, but his efforts did not produce. Food was scarce. He eventually lost more than sixty-five pounds. The days and nights began to grow brutally cold. After more than two months in the wilderness, Colter Barnes was starving to death. His physical movements became clumsy. His speech was slow and slurred. But he would not give in. Colter kept telling himself, "I gotta dig deep; I gotta dig deep."[1]

Chapter 8

The Deep Well Inside Us

Endurance is what you need now. . . . Then you will
receive all that he has promised.

> *"For in just a little while,*
> *the Coming One will come and not delay.*
> *And my righteous ones will live by faith.*
> *But I will take no pleasure in anyone who turns away."*

But we are not like those who turn away from God to
their own destruction. We are the faithful ones, whose
souls will be saved.

HEBREWS 10:36–39 NLT

Y ou are one of the faithful ones, dear reader. If you've
cared enough to make it this far through this book, I
can assure you—you are one of the faithful ones.

We are taking hold as best we can of the strength that prevails, the glory of God in us, so that we might have all we need to navigate these days victoriously. That strength, that beautiful, overcoming strength comes from the source of life himself, from Jesus Christ who dwells within us. It makes sense, then, that we would practice turning our attention to Jesus *within* us, learning to draw from his strength in the depths of our being.

It's important we remember that the strength that prevails is a strength given to us by God. This is not something we conjure up. It's not gritting our teeth and doubling down. You'll hear athletes talk of digging deep when some great contest is upon them. Soldiers use the same phrase, and it's good in the way it describes tapping into our deepest resources. But the similarity ends there, for the strength we are after is a *supernatural* strength that rises up from the God who not only created us but dwells within us.

"God is the strength of my heart and my portion forever" (Psalm 73:26). How wonderful, how life-changing it is to experience God as the strength of your heart!

We are talking about the beauty, strength, and glory of the oceans, forests, waterfalls, thunderstorms—all the wild power of creation. This is the power of God made available to us. Imagine if that beauty, strength, and glory not only dwelt within you but could be tapped into whenever you needed? Let your imagination go there for a moment.

The God of the open ocean dwells inside of me. His power is mine to draw upon.

This is Christianity as it could be:

For this reason I kneel before the Father, from whom
every family in heaven and on earth derives its name.
I pray that out of his glorious riches he may strengthen
you with power through his Spirit in your inner being.
(Ephesians 3:14–16)

Consider these passages from Ephesians in a couple of
other translations:

May He grant you out of the riches of His glory, to be
strengthened and spiritually energized with power
through His Spirit in your inner self, [indwelling your
innermost being and personality]. (v. 16 AMP)

Oh, the utter extravagance of his work in us who trust
him—endless energy, boundless strength! (1:19 THE
MESSAGE)

Don't allow your past experience to restrict your ability
to open yourself to this. Life is disappointing. There are
many things we don't understand, why God didn't come
through. I know this myself. But this is exactly why we
must allow the *Scriptures* to open new horizons for us, or we
will forever remain within the confines of our experience.
So think of it again: the God of shooting stars and swirling
galaxies, the Lord who sustains "all things by his powerful
word" (Hebrews 1:3) lives in you. What if you could draw
upon that glorious energy and power?

It would change things for sure.

In order to tap into that wild strength, we tap into God.

Like a tree sends its roots down deep into the subterranean world, we must learn to tap into the presence of God where he resides within us, deep in our inmost being.

Let's see if we can make this accessible.

Your Inmost Being

A few friends were sitting on our deck the other night talking about this and that when a woman we all know came up in the conversation. She's the kind of person who seems to have an internal steadiness. I don't think I've ever seen her thrown by anything. She might seem at first to be quiet and withdrawn, but that's only because she doesn't need to assert herself into the center of things. When she speaks, it seems to come from a deep resource. There was a moment of silence, and then someone said, "She's a deep well."

Actually, every human being is a deep well. They just don't draw upon those places within themselves because they live near the surface of their own existence. The madness of the world around us, with its incessant carnival of distraction and demand *is designed to keep you in the shallows*, by the way.[2]

Scripture clearly speaks of the depths of our inmost being as the place where God resides. This is a central theme of both the Old and New Testaments:

> Praise the LORD, my soul;
> all my inmost being, praise his holy name.
> (Psalm 103:1)

Like a tree sends its roots down

deep into the subterranean

world, we must learn to tap

into the presence of God

where he resides within us,

deep in our inmost being.

> The human spirit is the lamp of the LORD
> that sheds light on one's inmost being.
> (Proverbs 20:27)

> The one who believes in Me, as the Scripture said, "From his innermost being will flow rivers of living water." (John 7:38 NASB)

> Out of his glorious riches he may strengthen you with power through his Spirit in your inner being. (Ephesians 3:16)

You have an "inmost being," and this is where God dwells in you. So it makes sense that learning to tap into his deep presence will help us draw upon the strength that prevails.

> Your spirit instructs your soul that, since God is more present deep within you. . . . He must be sought within. And He must be enjoyed there. . . . Therefore, from the very beginning you find great joy in knowing that your Lord is within you and that you can find Him and enjoy Him in your inmost being.[3]

Now let me quickly clarify that this strength is available only to the sons and daughters of God, those who have invited him to come and reside in the center of their being. Until God resides *within* us, this is all magical thinking. There's lots of nonsense about inner resilience in little memes and quotes online. It doesn't work until Jesus of

Nazareth dwells inside of you. And so if you have not taken that step of faith, hope, and love, now would be a very good time to do so!

> *Oh Father, Jesus, Holy Spirit, I need you more than life itself. I'm incomplete without you. You are the source of my life and of every good thing I long for. I open my heart to you, Lord Jesus, and ask you to come and dwell in my innermost being. I surrender the rule of my life to you as Lord and Savior, and ask you to come and keep your promise—that if we open the door of our hearts, you will come and be one with us.*[4]

This is the secret of all recovery and resilience—that Jesus Christ himself comes to dwell within our created nature, deep down in the center of our being. And it is down in the depths that we must learn to tap into him, for the strength that prevails.

Simpler Than You Think

> *Jesus prayed intensely in public moments, sharing the liturgy of his people, but he also looked for select places, separated from the whirlwind of the world, places that allowed him to descend into the secret of his soul.*[5]

Now, I realize the idea of descending into the place where God dwells within us is probably new to most readers. It would *not* be new to the Christian monastic tradition for centuries, but most of us haven't had monastic training. So let's take it step by step; I think you'll discover this is quite accessible.

First, let's name the "levels" of our being:

- You have fleeting thoughts throughout the day, most of which are insignificant.
- You also have longings, hopes, and dreams that are far more important.
- Deep within you, you have experienced the cry for love, hope, and joy, which feels almost primal to your being.

I call these layers of our being the Shallows, Midlands, and Depths.

The Shallows of our being are characterized and ruled by the distractions of life. In the Shallows we flit from thought to thought, distraction to distraction almost unpredictably. You know how this goes—you're driving down the road listening to a podcast on the intelligence of dogs when the host makes a passing reference to his birthday. Your brain seizes on this little inconsequential remark, and you suddenly remember you forgot your mother's birthday, which leads to some panicked thoughts about how to make up for it and where you can buy a birthday card today. You think of the store that might have a card, and you recall that it's next to a great taco joint, which causes you to realize how much you love carnitas, and in a matter of a few nanoseconds you are miles from the actual topic of the podcast.

This is most people's mental life nowadays—a fluttering

array of randomly distracting thoughts flitting along like a thousand butterflies. Those are the Shallows of your existence.

The Midlands are characterized and ruled by what I, echoing Jesus' words, would call "the cares of life," the deeper worries, heartaches, longings, and aspirations that occupy the human heart (see Luke 21:34 and Matthew 4:19). Things like the health of your aging parents, the learning struggles of your children, the status of a troubled relationship, the progress of your career or lack thereof. Your finances, your own health, your hopes and fears for your future or the future of your loved ones.

I hope this helps you distinguish between the Midlands and the Shallows. The Midlands are deeper down in our being because they are the terrain of weightier matters. When Jesus said, "Watch yourselves, lest your hearts be weighed down with . . . the cares of this life" (Luke 21:34 ESV), this is the geography of heartache and fear he was referring to.

Distractions keep you in the Shallows for much of your day. They burn mental energy and take your focus on a roller coaster ride. But it is the pressures of the Midlands that keep you up at night—those are the things that cause us to pray, the things that give us ulcers. The Midlands, not the Shallows, tend to be the place of our tears.

Deeper still, down in the "depths of your being," is the essence of your existence, and the dwelling place of God (now that you have invited him to live in you!). The Depths are characterized and ruled by eternal things like faith, hope, love, and joy, to name a few. The prisoner sentenced to solitary confinement, the patient living out the final days of life in a lonely hospital room, and the castaway stranded on a remote island all discover that what once seemed so important now pales in the light of their longing to see their loved ones one more time.

We all have a deep inner life, whether we pay attention to it or not. This is very hopeful, because we *can* learn to access it.

How Do We Descend?

We are looking to find the presence of God in our inmost being, to experience him and commune with him there. By tapping into his actual presence within us, we are able to receive the strength that prevails. It begins with simply giving him your attention. As Theophan the Recluse instructed, "One must descend with the mind into the heart, and there stand before the face of the Lord, ever-present, all-seeing, within you."[6]

This is one of those quotes that sounds all profound and spiritual . . . but we don't really know what he's talking about. It seems beyond our experience, but I don't think it needs to be. The key idea here is the descending part. We learn to drop down into the presence of God within us, tap into his strength there.

When Theophan instructed us to "descend with the mind into the heart," I think by our "mind" he was referring to our conscious attention, and by "heart" he meant our inmost being, the Depths.

The psalmist cried out to God from his innermost being; he then gave the fullness of his attention to God:

> Out of the depths I cry to you, LORD;
> Lord, hear my voice.
> Let your ears be attentive
> to my cry for mercy. . . .
> I wait for the LORD, my whole being waits . . .
> I wait for the LORD
> more than watchmen wait for the morning,
> more than watchmen wait for the morning.
> (Psalm 130:1–2, 5–6)

Watchmen scan the horizon with careful attention, for their lives and the lives of the people within the city they protect depend on their attentiveness. The psalmist is using an analogy from his world to talk about *undistracted focus*: looking for God with all your attentiveness. It is something we give our whole being to. (You're going to love learning this, friends, and you're going to really love the fruit of it in your life.)

We set aside a time to give God our undivided attention (the battle is always for your attention). The new thought is that we are giving our attention to God-who-lives-within-us. As we tune out the world around us and tune in to our hearts, we become aware of the presence of Jesus-within-us. Take the experience of being comforted by God. Most of the time, nearly all of the time, that comfort is something we experience within. It might be facilitated by a comforting word or a passage of Scripture, but the comfort itself is taking place *within* us. There you go—you are tuning in to the work of God within you.

Finding God always begins with loving him.

Just begin to love Jesus, or your Father, or the Holy Spirit within you. *I love you, God. I love you, God. I love you.* Settle in, knowing you are taking it slowly. *I love you, God. I love you, God. I love you.* As we do this, we intentionally leave the distractions of the Shallows. We tune them out; we choose to ignore them. We begin to drop into our own being. As we consciously and intentionally love Jesus-within-us, it allows his Spirit to guide us into communion with him.

Because our attention is ruled 99 percent of the time by the Midlands and the Shallows, we have to get untangled from all that distraction to "descend." This is where benevolent detachment comes in—learning to give everyone and everything over to God. I explain this discipline in my book *Get Your Life Back*:

> We are aiming for release, turning over into the hands of God whatever is burdening us *and leaving it there.* It's so easy to get caught up in the drama in unhealthy ways, and then we are unable to see clearly, set boundaries, respond freely.[7]

> Cast all your anxiety on him because he cares for you. (1 Peter 5:7)

We're looking for a way to take back some healthy detachment in our lives.

Finding God always

begins with loving him.

You've got to release the world; you've got to release people, crises, trauma, intrigue, all of it. There has to be sometime in your day where you just let it all go. All the tragedy of the world, the heartbreak, the latest shooting, earthquake—the soul was never meant to endure this. The soul was never meant to inhabit a world like this. It's way too much. Your soul is finite. You cannot carry the sorrows of the world. Only God can do that. Only he is infinite. Somewhere, sometime in your day, you've just got to release it. You've got to let it go. . . .

Benevolent detachment takes practice. . . . "I give everyone and everything to you, God. I give everyone and everything to you." Often, I find I need to follow that up with some specifics: "I give my children to you," for I worry about them. "I give that meeting to you." "I give this book to you." As you do this, pay attention— your soul will tell you whether or not you're releasing. If the moment after you pray you find yourself mulling over the very thing you just released, you haven't released it. Go back and repeat the process until it feels that you have.[8]

This isn't about attaining some new level of sainthood. We're simply pausing, and releasing, and as we get the hang of it, we really do get better at letting go and leaving it "let go."

Descending to find God within us is a good time to practice benevolent detachment, because in this moment we are not asking our souls to let go of everything forever, only to let go for a few moments of focused prayer. I suppose mature saints are able to do it as a matter of living, but for our purposes we practice in order to find God in the depths of our being.

Cast all your cares upon him, as 1 Peter 5:7 urges us. We let go, surrender control, and withdraw from the world by putting it all in the hands of God for a few moments.

Give everyone and everything to me. This is how Jesus began to teach me to let go. So I repeat that phrase right back to him as my way of cooperating. *I give everyone and everything to you, God. I give everyone and everything to you.* This allows me to move my attention down into the depths of my being.

Most of us are unpracticed at drawing anything from the depths of our being because the tumultuous, upset world we live in constantly pulls, pushes, and distracts us, moment by moment keeping us on the surface of our life with God. But with practice you can ignore all that and find the beautiful presence of Jesus-within-you. Notice when you're praying—where is the God you are praying to *located*?

Are you praying to the Lord of the heavens up above?

Are you praying to Jesus who is always with you, by your side?

Or are you praying to Jesus who now lives in the depths of your own heart? The God who resides within you?

If you are looking to dig for deeper resources, you'll need to look deep within. Saint John of the Cross wrote a lovely poem about an angel coming to a man in desperate straits. The angel led him to a forest, and at a certain place told him to dig. He found buried treasure. John ended the poem by having the angel say to us, "Dig here, in your soul."

We ask the Holy Spirit to help us

"The Spirit searches all things, even the deep things of God. For who knows a person's thoughts except their own spirit within them?" (1 Corinthians 2:10–11)

The Spirit helps us in our weakness. We do not know what we ought to pray for, but the Spirit himself intercedes for us. . . . He who searches our hearts knows the mind of the Spirit, because the Spirit intercedes for God's people in accordance with the will of God. (Romans 8:26–27)

I pray something like this:

Holy Spirit, help me to descend.
Help me locate Christ in me.
Help me follow Christ down into the depths of my being.
I pray to commune with you there.

Your physical posture can help as well, especially early on. Once we are accustomed to it, we can practice going deeper just about anywhere—on the bus, in a plane, even during a meeting. But in the early stages of learning, you'll find it helpful to be in a quiet place and get your body into a position that enables you to turn your attention within. I like to sit in a favorite chair or lean against that chair while sitting on the floor, draw my knees up to my chest, and wrap my arms around my knees, bowing my head onto my arms, almost curling into a fetal position while I am sitting. This helps me physically shut out the world around me and begin to descend with my attention into my inner life.

As we settle into our attempt to give God-within-us our attention, we continue to simply love him, which allows our being to open to the reality of his presence. *I love you, I love you, I love you.*

(May I point out that simply giving Jesus lingering, undivided attention is going to be a new experience for most of us because we don't give *anything* our lingering, undivided attention these days. The exercise itself will begin to strengthen your ability to command your attention, which is a good thing in itself. The practice builds mental resilience.)

For me this began in this manner:

I would be in a simple time of prayer or quiet reflection, looking to give my attention to Jesus. As soon as I "found him" and tuned in to his presence with me, he would seem to recede from me. His presence seemed to draw back or draw deeper within. At first this was unsettling—why was my Lord retreating from my attempts to come close?

Rather than going to resignation and unbelief—that horrible little *I knew it* that resides in all of us—I asked him what was taking place. Jesus said, *Follow me.* Then I knew he was trying to get me to come deeper into my own being, to get out of the madness of the Shallows and the heartache of the Midlands in order to find a deeper experience of his presence within me.

Be merciful with your efforts. Many times I've been in a moment of genuine communion with God-within-me when suddenly I'm yanked back to the Shallows by some distraction, or pulled to the Midlands by some care. Do not be distressed by this; it's very common. The entire world is shouting at you all the time, trying to capture your attention, and we are unfamiliar with lingering communion with God. Be kind to yourself by simply acknowledging, *Oh, I got yanked back to the surface.* And drop back down again.

What will you find, as you find Jesus-in-the-depths-of-you?

Friends, you will find such goodness, expressed personally to your need in that moment.

You will find love. Often your experience will simply be one of being loved, of knowing God's love for you. Linger with that; it is enough. (When I'm having a hard time "dropping in," I will often use the trail of love. I find where the longing for love lies within me, and I follow it to Jesus, like Hansel and Gretel following the bread crumbs home. It leads to Jesus, who always lives in the place of love in our innermost being.)

Other times, Jesus has instructed me to find my longing for hope (again, never too far out of reach) and follow the longing for hope down into my inner being.

As we commune with God's presence within us, we are able to receive the strength that prevails. His glorious resilience is always available to us. Simply lingering in the presence of Jesus-within-us strengthens us. The communion is the point. Remember, just because these are supernatural graces doesn't mean they are dramatic. Don't look for fireworks and explosions. God is gentle. Receiving his love and strength is often a gentle experience.

Sometimes we find that God wants to say something to us, or show us something. Give him your attention.

Holy Spirit, help me hear what Jesus is saying to me.

Holy Spirit, help me see what Jesus is showing me.

I have had hundreds of beautiful encounters with Jesus through this practice. He has shown me the new earth. Seeing its beauty, seeing the utter victory of it was healing in itself and filled me with assurance. He has shown me the city of God, filled with laughter and joy. It increased my longing to be there.

Just go with what Jesus is doing; each experience tends to be unique.

Skill
DESCENDING TO FIND JESUS-WITHIN-YOU

Find a quiet place. In a busy home even the bathroom or a closet will work because you can shut the door. Do not bring your phone. If you need it for a timer or for music, put it on airplane mode. Get your body into a comfortable position, like pulling your knees up to your chest and wrapping your arms around your knees. I don't recommend lying down because you'll fall asleep (we are all so weary). Sometimes a comfy blanket can assist you in "settling in."

I will play soft, instrumental music in the background on occasion, but *only* as a backdrop to create a sacred space, not as something asking for my attention. No lyrics—only gentle, quiet instrumental music.*

Start with a simple prayer:

Jesus, I long for your presence, Lord. Help me commune with you where you live inside of me.

Repeat that several times over. Repetition is really helpful in this kind of prayer. I'll repeat things over and over as I tune in.

As you quiet yourself, practice benevolent detachment.

Jesus, I give everyone and everything to you, God.

I give everyone and everything to you.

Repeat that a few times. If something keeps trying to distract you, specifically give the issue over to God:

I give you my children, my work, that email.

But don't get caught up in a whole laundry-list of cares. Just ignore the Shallows and keep tuning in to Jesus-within-you. Ask the Holy Spirit for his help.

Holy Spirit, help me to descend.

Help me locate Christ in me.

Help me follow Christ down into the depths of my being.

I pray to commune with you there.

Begin loving Jesus, or your Father, or the Holy Spirit *within you* (not looking to the Lord above, nor to Christ by your side, but looking within).

I love you, God. I love you, God. I love you.

Settle in, knowing you are taking it slowly.

I love you, God. I love you, God. I love you.

Become aware of Jesus-within-you, and follow him deeper within.

---

* "Soaking in His Presence" by William Augusto is a favorite of ours for this purpose.

Be open to what he wants to do. It might be comfort, it might be a word from God, or he might want to show you something. Let him take the lead.

This is not a time for typical prayer. Don't start praying for the cares you hold up in the Midlands. Don't intercede for others. This precious time is dedicated to one thing only—communion with God. As you linger there, ask God for his glorious strength.

Father, Jesus, Holy Spirit, fill the depths of my being with your glory. Fill me with your glory, Lord. Fill me with the river of life in my inmost being. Let the river flow in me. Give me the strength that prevails, Lord. Fill me with your glorious strength. I pray for supernatural resilience.

TIRED DECISION-MAKERS = DANGEROUS DECISIONS

The fall itself took only seconds.

Four climbers, roped together, were descending from the summit of Mount Hood on May 30, 2002, using ice axes and crampons. They had finished the grueling five-hour climb with high-fives at the summit; now it was time to get off the mountain. For some reason they decided to pull their fixed protection—their anchor of safety—and were attempting to walk down while roped only to one another, a string of weary men held to the ice by the tiny points of their crampons.

The top man slipped and fell. With thirty-five feet of rope between him and the climber below, he had fallen seventy feet before the rope went taut. That's like falling off a seven-story building. He was going at least thirty miles per hour when he yanked the second man off and the speed and force multiplied from there with irreversible consequence. All four climbers were ripped from the mountain. As they plummeted toward the crevasse, the swirling tangle clotheslined two more teams of climbers, sweeping them all into the abyss. Three climbers died that day.

Why would they descend in such a risky manner? As Laurence Gonzales wrote in Deep Survival,

> *Most climbers reach the summit tired, dehydrated, hypoxic, hypoglycemic, and sometimes hypothermic. Any one of those factors would be enough to erode mental and physical abilities. Put together, they make you clumsy, inattentive, and accident-prone. They impair judgment.[1]*

Chapter 9

Your Prescription

Then the Kingdom of Heaven will be like ten bridesmaids who took their lamps and went to meet the bridegroom. Five of them were foolish, and five were wise. The five who were foolish didn't take enough olive oil for their lamps, but the other five were wise enough to take along extra oil. When the bridegroom was delayed, they all became drowsy and fell asleep. At midnight they were roused by the shout, "Look, the bridegroom is coming! Come out and meet him!" All the bridesmaids got up and prepared their lamps. Then the five foolish ones asked the others, "Please give us some of your oil because our lamps are going out."

MATTHEW 25:1–8 NLT

I think most readers find this parable unnerving and unclear—somebody gets left out of the wedding feast in the New Eden because they ran out of *olive oil*?! What does that mean? How do we avoid it?

In some cases, Jesus went on to interpret his parables, but not this one. The absence of interpretation is intriguing, because this is one of the parables Jesus told right after his penultimate warnings about the end of the age. Maybe he *meant* it to be unnerving; maybe Jesus wants us to sit up and pay attention.

Whatever else the parable of the ten bridesmaids means, the lesson surely includes this: We need to renew our love and devotion to Jesus, our deep union with him. We need to make sure we don't run out of love and devotion and the resilience God-within-us provides before he returns.

Because I think the precious oil is God-within-us.

Throughout the Scriptures the Holy Spirit is connected with oil. We know we are meant to be filled with the Spirit, with God's presence. If we add to that the reality C. S. Lewis pointed out, that God is the fuel the human soul runs on, I think the parable makes sense.

> God made us: invented us as a man invents an engine. . . .
> Now God designed the human machine to run on
> Himself. He Himself is the fuel our spirits were designed
> to burn, or the food our spirits were designed to feed on.[2]

But of course—God is the fountain of life. We are only empty vessels, needing a source of life. It is Jesus-within-us that gives us resilience. I think what happened to those unfortunate bridesmaids is that they ran out of God! They didn't see to it that they were filled with God, and when things wore on through the night, they ran out.

Let's make sure we are filled with God. It requires *intention*; the parable is clear about that.

Summing up all we have covered thus far, here's our situation as best we know it:

1. We've all been softened, weakened, robbed of resilience from years of living in the Comfort Culture. (Our biggest crisis was something like a long line at Starbucks or our phone battery dying.)
2. Then came global trauma in the years of the pandemic and its sociodramas. So we are depleted and beat up.
3. We are in trauma rehab now, and we need to take that rehab seriously. Pretending everything is back to normal is delusional.
4. We're therefore in an especially vulnerable place right now. Desolation and other predatory forces are trying to make us give up, lose heart, abandon our faith, or simply give our hearts to comforters other than God.

Jesus urges us toward endurance, resilience. It's available in him. But it won't just happen. We must take hold of the strength that prevails.

So—what's your plan to make it through?

You need a plan, dear ones. Resilience and victory aren't going to come with a swipe on your home screen.

Honestly, it can be as simple as this adjustment:

The world really has gone mad.
I'm not going to get pulled down with it.

You need a plan. Resilience

and victory aren't going

to come with a swipe on

your home screen.

I'm readjusting my life around recovery and resilience;
this is my orientation now.

People do this all the time—we adjust our lives to make room for the birth of a child, or for a career change, or to pursue a degree, or a dream, or simply to take up cycling. Given everything we've covered in this book so far, I'm suggesting we adjust our lives to provide recovery from the past and build resilience for the days ahead.

But I'm in a real bind.

I want to make suggestions that I know would be truly helpful. I also recognize that most folks feel as though they have no margin—emotionally, mentally, or in any other way. The last thing I want to do is increase your load.

So let me first say this—if you do nothing else, and you want recovery and resilience, I would strongly recommend two things:

1. **First, renew your love and devotion to Jesus.** Give time each day to loving him. This deepens your union and allows you to draw upon the life of Jesus-within-you. So simple, but most folks don't even spend five minutes a day simply loving Jesus. They don't know what they're missing.
2. **Second, create a little margin in your life to allow your soul room to breathe.** You can't just keep slogging on; you have to make room for recovery and resilience. It can start with five to ten minutes, morning and evening. A few evenings each week where you aren't doing anything. A day off now and then.

And in that margin, in the space you create, you ask for the supernatural graces. You ask for attachment, the strength that prevails, the glory of God, the river of life. Descend into your innermost being and commune with Jesus there. I promise you, these two things will make a world of difference in your life.

My team and I have developed an app to help you with these simple practices—it's called "30 Days to Resilience." This beautiful, guided experience allows you to pause morning, noon, and night to recenter yourself in Jesus, pray, hear scripture read to you, and rest as you listen to beautiful music. It only takes a few minutes, but it is *so* refreshing. You can find "30 Days to Resilience" on our "One Minute Pause" app available in the App Store. Simply search for the app and download it for free. Then give the experience a try.

Now—if you want to take your resilience a little more seriously, I have a two-part prescription to share with you. The first part focuses on the practical patterns of life that will help you with recovery from the trauma we've experienced, not just through the pandemic but over the course of any human life. The second part digs a little deeper into developing resilience—the inner resources to face future trials.

Part One: Embracing Recovery

Athletes will tell you that working out is not the most important part of training. Recovery is. The number one cause of athletic injuries is the lack of recovery time between training sessions.[3]

Let me repeat this because it's so counterintuitive—recovery is more important to athletic performance than training is. Your body needs to rest and repair between periods of exertion. "By not letting each of the muscle groups rest, a person will reduce their ability to repair. Insufficient rest also slows fitness progression and increases the risk of injury."[4]

That's very orienting. It's a physical expression of a reality that applies to your heart and soul as well. We could probably predict who's going to burn out and who's not by looking at their recovery practices.

But most people don't take their recovery seriously. They're simply shocked and heartbroken when their soul suddenly gives out, like a camel who has walked a thousand miles and drops. How will you build recovery into your life? What's your plan?*

Healing from trauma involves naming what the trauma was, and what its effects upon us have been. This is the "story work" every good therapist helps their client through: What happened? What was it like? Tell me the story. (This "narrative approach" helps process trauma and rewires the brain.)[5]

As we were turning the corner from December 2020 into January 2021, many of my friends were making plans and setting goals for the new year. There was a lot of anticipation at that time about a new year. The commonly heard

---

* In many ways this book is part 2 of a conversation on resiliency and the healing of our humanity. Part 1 is called *Get Your Life Back: Everyday Practices for a World Gone Mad*. That book will give you many practical things to do for recovery, simple things like learning to pause in your day; allowing your soul transition time between one thing and the next; and understanding the healing power of nature and beauty.

phrase was, "I just want 2020 to be over." But 2021 turned out to look a whole lot like 2020 in most parts of the world. Still, we clung to whatever optimism we could.

I just couldn't do it. I usually look forward to dreaming about a new year, but my soul simply wouldn't cooperate. It had to do with *grief*.

There were so many losses and sources of heartbreak in 2020 I simply couldn't move on without attending to them. I had to sit down with a pad of paper and begin to put words to all I had suffered, as if I were talking to a therapist about a traumatic event. One by one I had to name my losses. I needed to honor my soul by allowing for the fact that these *were* real losses (a hard thing to do when everyone else is acting "fine"). I needed to name my sorrows and then grieve them, allowing the sadness to come forth and express itself.

You can't heal trauma without grieving it. This is why the mad rush to grab some joy and the global denial insisting that "things are getting back to normal" are cruel to the soul. It's a shared attempt to sweep it all under the rug, but the problem is a good part of your soul goes right along with it. Under the rug.

I want to suggest two things:

1. **First, look back to name what these years have been like for you.** Name the losses, the fears, the sources of your anger and frustration. Imagine I'm your therapist and I've just asked you:

   • What's it been like for you?
   • What's been hard?

- What made you mad?
- What do you wish had never happened?

Put it all out there. Honor it. Grieve it.

2. **Second, pay attention in the current moment**. It's far better to do this in real time—name what the current moment feels like, what it's demanding of you, how it's impacting your soul. Stay current with the cost of living in an hour like this. When you have a heart for humanity, when you share Jesus' compassion for people, communities, and creation, you're going to experience a lot of heartache in an hour like this one. Care for your soul by putting words to what it's like. Don't just pretend everything is fine.

By the way, this is exactly what is modeled for us in the Psalms—David and the other writers cry out to God with deeply raw descriptions of what is happening all around them, and how it makes them feel. Read Psalms 6, 13, and 42 for examples. Let them be your guide to emotional health.

Practice benevolent detachment—giving it all over to Jesus, every single day. As the world spins into greater and greater madness and denial, I've found myself more and more upset. Jesus keeps saying to me, *Give it all to me.*

Yes, Lord. I release it all to you. Only you can save.

Replenishing Reserves

Your plan also needs to make adjustments to replenish your reserves.

Remember—we tap into our reserves in order to rally. Even good things like weddings and the birth of a child tap into reserves. We have all rallied; we have all had to dig deep. Now we need to give some care to our reserves.

The math is simple: reserves are replenished when there's more coming *in* than there is going *out*.

That's how it works. That's why people come back from their vacations feeling better, and why folks who have taken real time off, like a sabbatical, come back almost different human beings. Your reserve tanks don't just magically fill up, no more than your car's gas tank does. They definitely don't replenish when you're burning everything just to maintain what you call your "normal life." That's why you make a *plan* for recovery and resilience.

You'll want to arrange for periods where more is coming in than is going out.

Whatever your operating capacity is—whether that's currently 40 percent, 60 percent, or 95 percent of what used to be your full capacity—your *current* operating capacity is what you need to pay attention to. You need to throttle back to allow your reserves to fill back up.

I hear the objections at once: *But you don't know my life! You don't know what my boss is asking of me! What my kids need right now!* I completely understand. We are all hard-pressed, some of us more than others. But there's a way to account for even this.

We burn through so much of our emotional, mental, and spiritual energy simply through worry, anger, being generally unsettled, and by taking in too much of the overwhelming news of the world. Picture a gambler standing before a slot machine and repeatedly, almost mindlessly, dropping in silver dollar after silver dollar. Soon she has nothing left in her purse and nothing to show for it. The sociodrama of the world is the slot machine; the silver dollars represent our personal resources. We spend it all like the gambler until we choose to walk away.

Friends, you can turn and walk away. Without needing one more day of vacation or some ideal work schedule, you can walk away from a whole lot of what is currently draining you.

I beg of you—practice benevolent detachment.

We do need to provide for periods in the rhythm of our week, month, and year where we are *intentionally* operating below our capacity to replenish reserves. It doesn't have to be limited to your vacation time. It's something you can build into the rhythm of your life. Which evenings each week are blocked out in your calendar? You should block several out: no activity, no nothin'. Turn your phone off, and let your soul simply rest.

God commands Sabbath once a week however you observe it, and I think now you can see the brilliance of his command. We need margin to replenish, margin that is so protected it is sacred margin—untouchable, nonnegotiable.

The simplest (and by far the most reliable) route I have ever found for getting breathing room in my life is to begin asking Jesus about the plans I make for my life.

+ Do I really need to have my folks over for dinner?
+ Do I really need to repaint that spare room this weekend?
+ Do I really need to call this person back this evening?

We need margin to replenish,

margin that is so protected

it is sacred margin—

untouchable, nonnegotiable.

Honestly, I'm always startled at how much feels to me to be utterly necessary, unavoidable—but when I asked Christ about it, he rescued me from the pressure. I didn't need to make that call that evening. I didn't need to do that project that weekend. I didn't need to get involved in someone else's drama even though I felt I should.

Jesus has consistently opened up margin in my life that I didn't think was possible. And in that margin I have been able to recover and replenish my reserves.

The Surprising Importance of Play

During the height of the pandemic and the daily barrage of death counts and mounting social tension, God brought me a surprising source of recovery.

Spikeball.

It's a game played with four players circling a round net, which sits on a frame about eight inches off the ground. The players are divided into two teams of two. You ricochet the bouncy rubber ball off the net to the opposing team with a good solid whack, hoping the opponents cannot return the volley. Like any game there are rules that make it harder and thus more fun. The more you get into it, the more you risk life and limb to save a shot or make a fabulous play.

My colleagues and I would retreat to the parking lot behind our building at least once a day and get into a rousing game of Spikeball. Every single time I came back to my desk, I had a smile on my face. I felt refreshed, renewed. It seemed silly to be playing Spikeball when the world was falling apart, but Jesus knew this was the very reason we needed play in our lives.

Author and journalist Sebastian Junger was embedded with a forward position platoon at the height of the war in Afghanistan. These young soldiers, barely men, were stationed in the Korengal Valley, notoriously difficult to occupy. Various platoons would take turns occupying the farthest outpost, surrounded by mountain cliffs and murderous enemy fighters. It was common for them to be fired upon from multiple angles above them at any given moment. I can hardly imagine a more trying survival situation.

What struck me in Junger's harrowing narrative is how these soldiers out on the fringes of survival would suddenly break into rounds of spontaneous horseplay in the small gravel yard of this remote and wildly exposed position:

> Choking guys out was considered fine sport, so soldiers tended to keep their backs to something so no one could sneak up from behind. Jumping someone was risky because everyone was bound by affiliations that broke down by platoon, by squad, and finally by team. If a man in your squad got jumped by more than one guy you were honor-bound to help out. . . . That meant that within seconds you could have ten or fifteen guys in a pile on the ground.[6]

It's a story repeated throughout the history of men at war or in dire situations like it—they play sports, they gamble, they play video games for hours if they can get them. When Shackleton and his crew found themselves utterly stranded on the fringes of Antarctica (their ship completely crushed), they played soccer out on the ice.

Toward the end of his life, C. S. Lewis became very ill. He was forced to resign from Cambridge, a heartbreak for him. He also required a live-in male nurse whom he only sort of tolerated. Lewis had his many books brought home to his little cottage. One day, while his nurse napped, Lewis and Walter Hooper built a wall of books around the sleeping man, who woke utterly startled to find himself imprisoned floor to ceiling. I love that Lewis retained his sense of humor till the end.[7]

Play is a way of keeping perspective, of lightening up. Laurence Gonzales wrote in *Deep Survival*,

> Some high-angle [mountaineering] rescue workers call body bags "long-term bivvy sacks." It sounds cruel, but survivors laugh and play, and even in the most horrible situations—perhaps especially in those situations—they continue to laugh and play. To deal with reality you must first recognize it as such, and . . . play puts a person in touch with his environment, while laughter makes the feeling of being threatened manageable.[8]

Here I am writing a book on what very well could be *the* pinnacle moments of history and the intense trials they usher in, but about every thirty minutes I need to go out in the yard and chuck the ball for my golden retrievers. You just can't live in the intensity. The human soul needs play, especially in times like these.

Where are you getting some play back in your life? Play helps with recovery *and* resilience. Don't you just love God for that?

Part Two: Embracing Resilience

We also need to rearrange our lives to develop *resilience*—mentally, emotionally, spiritually.

Mental Resilience

Mental resilience begins when we decide to take hold of our thought life.

Start with speculation, something we all indulge in. And I do mean *indulge*. Speculation is like a wild horse running wherever it wants—without bridle, halter, or any sort of restraint—and we just let it run wild. We do it in our personal lives: *Why didn't Julie return my text? She must be mad at me. Maybe I should call her, maybe she doesn't want to be friends anymore, maybe it was what I said last week* . . . We do it on a global level: *Oh man, where is this world headed? What kind of world are my children or grandchildren going to inherit? Do we need to stockpile food? Bury gold in the backyard?*

Speculation is draining. Did you know it's also something Jesus banned? "Therefore do not worry about tomorrow, for tomorrow will worry about itself. Each day has enough trouble of its own" (Matthew 6:34).

"Do not worry" is a command, not a suggestion.

I think most of us look at speculation as a personal weakness, like biting our fingernails or compulsively glancing at our phones. But I bet you haven't seen it as a violation of faith, hope, and love. It is.

You can start building mental resilience right here, by roping in speculation. Every time you find yourself speculating, tell yourself to *stop it!* Bring your thoughts back under

---

"Do not worry" is a command,

not a suggestion.

---

control: *I'm not indulging speculation. It's godless.* Turn your thoughts immediately to God: *You are good, Father. You are with me. You are still in control.* Putting a bridle on speculation builds mental resilience.

By the way, this is going to go a lot easier for you if you get off social media and what is called the "news." In chapter 2 we talked about who is shaping the narrative for you right now, who is shaping your perspective on the world. Only Jesus should get that place in your life. We concluded that it's better to give more of your attention to the story God is telling than to any form of media you consume, especially social media. Good heavens—when the data shows a direct correlation between rising rates of anxiety and depression with the amount of time you spend on social media, why do you spend any time there at all? I know it sounds arcane, but the friends of mine who are the happiest are the same folks who dropped all their social media accounts.

Navy SEAL training includes teaching the recruits positive self-talk. Apparently we say something like three hundred to one thousand words to ourselves every minute. You know from experience that a whole bunch of it is negative. Mental resilience is built by intentionally, consciously saying positive things—which for the believer would be all the beautiful truths of Scripture. *God is with me. I am secure. Christ lives within me. I have the strength that prevails.* Positive self-talk helps calm fears aroused by the amygdala, that part of the brain that governs anxiety.[9]

In recent days I've found myself driving along reciting out loud the opening lines from the Apostles' Creed: "I believe in God, the Father Almighty, creator of heaven and earth. I believe in Jesus . . ."

So simple, but so very helpful. *This is what I believe; this is what I believe.*

Reading and memorizing scripture builds mental resilience because it is a living, breathing text in which you encounter God, and through which you get perspective on the world. How good would it be for your mental health to be reminded each day that Jesus is Lord of all, "running the universe, everything from galaxies to governments, no name and no power exempt from his rule" (Ephesians 1:20–21 THE MESSAGE). Try reading Isaiah 40 for five days in a row and watch what it does for your soul.

Skill
A PRAYER FOR MENTAL RESILIENCE

Begin with three deep breaths.

Search me, God, and know my heart . . . know my anxious thoughts (Psalm 139:23).

I come to you, Jesus, for peace of mind. I give my mind to you. I set my mind on you. Capture my every thought. I surrender all the news. All worry and speculation. I surrender everything grabbing my attention.

I give you my thoughts, Jesus. All of my mental life: my focus and attention, my memory and recall, my understanding and imagination. I dedicate the life of my mind to you, Lord Jesus, and you alone.

The mind governed by God's Spirit is life and peace (Romans 8:6). Holy Spirit, Spirit of God, come and fill my mind. Come and fill my thoughts. Fill my mind with life and peace.

Repeat that . . .

Holy Spirit, Spirit of God, come and fill my mind. Come and fill my thoughts. Fill my mind with life and peace.

For we have the mind of Christ (1 Corinthians 2:16). I pray to be one mind with you, Jesus. One thought, one imagination, one mental life. I receive the mind of Christ. I receive the mind of Christ.

Fix your thoughts on what is true, and honorable, right and pure, lovely and admirable. Think about things that are excellent and worthy of praise (Philippians 4:8). Think about something beautiful, something that reminds you of the goodness of God. A place you love. A sweet memory. Something in nature. Something that makes you smile.

Now stay with that today.†

---

† This prayer is taken from the "One Minute Pause" app; within that app are several life-giving "pauses" and prayers. Two of those are "Mental Strength"

Emotional Resilience

Mental resilience helps build emotional resilience.

I've been a Christian therapist for almost thirty years, and I believe in the importance of allowing ourselves the full range of our emotions. I just encouraged you to name and grieve the losses and pressures you face, so I'm not some hard-core drill instructor when I also say, *You cannot let your emotions drive the bus.*

Years in the Comfort Culture made us emotionally soft.

If we don't feel like doing something, we don't do it.

If we don't feel like believing something, we don't believe it.

Folks like to call this authenticity, but it's really just adolescence. Like a fourteen-year-old, we treat our emotions as some sort of right, the truest part of our existence. If we don't feel love, we think we are no longer in love; if we don't feel God, we think maybe he's not around anymore. We coddle our feelings when what we need to do is bring them under the rule of Christ, just like our thought life. We build emotional resilience by not letting them control our perspective or our reaction to things. Simply because fear sweeps over you in the night doesn't mean you have to give way to it.

The Norwegian explorer Roald Amundsen is regarded as one of the great polar explorers. In 1911 he was first to reach the South Pole. As a boy Amundsen would sleep with his bedroom windows open during winter to develop resilience.[10] I like that picture, of toughening ourselves up after years in the Comfort Culture.

---

pauses. You can download the app free from the App Store.

Two of the climbers who were swept off the face of Mount Hood in the story I shared at the beginning of this chapter were running partners—Chris Kern and Harry Slutter. When things got painful during the races they ran together, they would say to each other, "Put away the pain and hold on!" They didn't just stop running, and this practice of emotional control saved them during the accident. As the nine injured and dying climbers tried to untangle themselves in the crevasse, Kern was screaming. He had broken his pelvis. But the screaming was sending shock waves through the entire group, and in that moment they needed every bit of mental clarity they could get. Slutter yelled at him, "Put away the pain and hold on!" Kern got quiet and began repeating the phrase to himself.[11]

We honor our emotions by acknowledging them. We *bridle* our emotions by keeping them subject to truth.

Let me remind you here of the importance of our attachment to God. Emotional fortitude is not based in severity but in *security*. As Mark Matousek wrote in an article for *Psychology Today*, "Having found a secure base in the world, according to psychologist John Bowlby, the founder of attachment theory, the child learns emotional resilience."[12] We operate from a base of love and acceptance, blessing and assurance.

Remember—when Jesus tells us "don't be alarmed," "don't let your heart be troubled," "be on guard so that your hearts are not weighed down,"[13] he's loving us and treating us like grown-ups, assuming that we can control our emotions.

You say something you regret. You drop the ball on a project. You feel terrible. But you say to yourself, *Just*

We honor our emotions by
acknowledging them. We
bridle our emotions by keeping
them subject to truth.

---

because I made a mistake doesn't mean I'm a failure. I am deeply loved. I am accepted in Christ. I'm telling you—this sort of emotional resilience changes your life.

And it is absolutely vital when it comes to the sweeping forces of the Falling Away I spoke of earlier. As the world turns further and further from God, you will be sorely tempted to surrender some of your core convictions, if not all of them. The temptation will come over your emotions, your feelings—it doesn't feel like God is listening; it doesn't feel like he's coming through. You must not let those emotions undermine your faith. Honestly, in an hour like this one, we have to imitate the mental, emotional, and spiritual resilience Daniel and his companions showed in the face of enormous pressure:

> Then Nebuchadnezzar, in rage and fury, gave the command to bring Shadrach, Meshach, and Abed-Nego. So they brought these men before the king. Nebuchadnezzar spoke, saying to them, "Is it true, Shadrach, Meshach, and Abed-Nego, that you do not serve my gods or worship the gold image which I have set up? Now if you are ready at the time you hear the sound of the horn . . . and you fall down and worship the image which I have made, good! But if you do not worship, you shall be cast immediately into the midst of a burning fiery furnace. And who is the god who will deliver you from my hands?"
>
> Shadrach, Meshach, and Abed-Nego answered and said to the king, "O Nebuchadnezzar, we have no need to answer you in this matter. If that is the case, our God whom we serve is able to deliver us from the burning

fiery furnace, and He will deliver us from your hand, O king. But if not, let it be known to you, O king, that we do not serve your gods, nor will we worship the gold image which you have set up." (Daniel 3:13–18 NKJV)

"But if not . . ." In other words, "No." Simply *No—I'm not surrendering to the culture or any other pull to compromise my love for God and my allegiance to him. No.* This is going to be critical against every form of Desolation—you simply cannot give it running room.

Skill
DO NOT LET YOUR HEARTS BE WEIGHED DOWN!

But be on your guard, so that your hearts will not be weighed down with dissipation and drunkenness and the worries of life, and that this day will not come on you suddenly, like a trap; for it will come upon all those who live on the face of all the earth. But stay alert at all times, praying that you will have strength to escape all these things that are going to take place, and to stand before the Son of Man. (Luke 21:34–36 NASB)

Oh friends, there is such compassion and understanding here; there is also wisdom and instruction for our escape! We all feel weighed down. (When was the last time you had days of feeling completely lighthearted?) The Greek word for "weighed down" is *bareo*, which means "to burden, weigh down, depress."[14] Yep. I've been right there. Burdened by the "worries of life," which we have more than enough of coming at us. We are hard-pressed on every side, and our hearts are being weighed down. The good news is, if Jesus warned us about it, then he believed there was a way out. "Weighed down" does not have to be our fate; it is not inevitable. Really.

Emotional resilience is saying,

Jesus, I consecrate my emotional life to you. I consecrate all of my feelings. I bring them under your rule and into alignment with you. I pray to be one heart and one mind with you. I invite your Spirit into my emotional life. I ask you for the strength that prevails here—in my emotional life. I receive your hope, Jesus. I receive your joy. I receive your courage. I bring my emotional life under the rule of Jesus Christ and Jesus Christ alone. I refuse to let this world get me spun up. I refuse to let it make me fearful or angry. I refuse to take the bait. When I need to grieve, Lord, I grieve in you. When I need to get mad, I get mad in you.

You are in control, Lord. You are still running the universe. And I trust you. I give everyone and everything to you, Lord. I declare that all things shall be mine at your return.

Plan for the "Dailies"

Now let me say what I really need to say, what we all need to hear right now.

The mistake folks are making in this rough hour is trying to figure out how to fit a little more of God into their crowded lives.

We need to do the opposite. Start with God, center your life on him, and work outward from there. Our spirituality moves from something that is *part* of our life to the *epicenter* of our life—from which all other things flow, and to which all other plans yield.

Plan to become the most converted person your friends and family know. So why don't we go ahead and call this the new monasticism—rearranging our days to be centered around our life in God, drawing upon his strength for our resilience. It's the only way we're going to make it.

> [Daniel] went home and knelt down as usual in his upstairs room, with its windows open toward Jerusalem. He prayed three times a day, just as he had always done, giving thanks to his God. (Daniel 6:10 NLT)

"Just as he had always done"—in other words, this was his normal routine, not an exceptional moment. The resilience Daniel showed in a dark culture (and in the lions' den) was built in his daily practices. Pausing to pray morning, noon, and night was habitual for him. And that's the key—it's the things that become habitual that shape our lives.

If we have made God our priority and we have a history of tapping into him, then we are in a much better position to draw upon his resilience when crisis comes. If we have tinkered with our spiritual life, if it has *not* been a priority, troubled times wake us up and urge us to prioritize God now.

We need some new habits (or the recollection of old habits) that fit within our daily routine. Let me quickly add that whatever we take on now to help with our recovery and resilience *has to be realistic or we won't sustain it.* Here's something simple and sustainable: set your phone alarm so that three times a day you stop, love God, and give him your allegiance.

I love you, God. I love you, God. I love you.

I give you my allegiance. I choose you over all things.

Give me the strength that prevails.

I think a daily "declaration of faith" is a good idea. If you recite the Apostles' Creed every day for five days, I guarantee you it will brighten your perspective. Or you could make a copy of what I did with Psalm 23 on pages 36 and 37 and make it part of your daily declaration!

You can also adopt a few simple phrases that remind you of the core truths of your life with God, and what he is offering you. For example, if a simple phrase like "I am loved, I am chosen, I am safe in the arms of God" works for you, if it resonates in such a way that it's always right there, then you can use it multiple times a day to anchor your mental and emotional life.

I love the phrase "your glory, your love, your kingdom" because it helps me to invoke the glory of God that we talked about, the power of his love in a world filled with hate, and the supremacy of his kingdom over the false kingdoms of this world. It has become second nature for me to declare "your glory, your love, your kingdom" throughout my day, especially when I feel my mental or emotional life beginning to spin.

Let me suggest a few other simple things that could become habitual for you, and thus immensely life-giving . . .

WORSHIP

Over the years Stasi and I enjoyed an evening now and then simply playing worship music in our living room while we turned our hearts toward Jesus. Even though we never, ever regretted making room for it, we also never made it a regular practice. (What *is* it with human nature?) But the pressures of this global moment have driven us to make it almost daily. (I say "almost daily" to be honest, and because fitting it in five evenings a week is still a vast improvement!)

Worship does all sorts of wonderful things for your heart and soul, and for your union with Christ. Worship catches our mental life and turns it toward Jesus. It builds resilience because we are staying focused on God for twenty or thirty minutes. It opens our spirit to him, allowing us to receive his love, comfort, and the strength that prevails. Worship is also a declaration of faith—declaring the goodness of God, who he is, what he's done. (And the demons absolutely hate it, so it's a great form of spiritual warfare!)

I suggest bedtime, but you can also fit this into a morning or evening commute, if you have space to do so. Play worship music while making dinner or cleaning up. You can fit it in. For us, twenty to thirty minutes of worship fits nicely before bedtime, followed by our bedtime prayers.

Which brings us to prayer.

PRAYER

I strongly urge you to take up Daniel's practice of morning, noon, and evening prayers. Stasi and I don't leave the house in the morning or even have breakfast until we've prayed our morning prayers. (Most often we pray individually because we rise at different times and need personal connection with Jesus before anything else.) Our evening prayers we share together before bedtime.

The "30 Days to Resilience" experience will help you put all this to practice in a simple way each day—make sure to download the "One Minute Pause" app!

What else would be wise to make part of your dailies?

Here's a fun exercise: If you *could* become a monk, what is the lifestyle you see yourself living? (Come on, we've all dreamed about unplugging from our jobs, running away from it all, living in some beautiful place at a soulful pace.) What would you do if you could have that life? What would it involve as a daily rhythm? Quiet, prayer, meditation, walks, simple work like baking bread?

Honestly, you can incorporate most of that into your normal life. You can take an evening walk; you can enjoy making meals.

Your Plan Is Your Prescription

If you want to be among those who do not run out of God at the end of things, you should write yourself a prescription for your new monastic life. Your life of recovery and resilience. I'm dead serious. You know your strengths and weaknesses; what do you need to do to take the strength of your soul seriously at this time?

I strongly recommend you also ask Jesus for your prescription in this hour.

I did this for the summer of 2021. I knew I was beat up

and probably overestimating my capacity. I had a window for some sabbath, a slower pace of life, and though everything in me wanted to travel and go on adventures, I asked Jesus what I needed.

First we had to work through my insistence that lots of adventure travel was what I needed. He kept saying *no* (and I will quickly admit that after that time of rest, I was very grateful he had said *no*).

"What do I need, Lord?"

- Simplicity. Keep this summer very simple.
- Beauty.
- Walks.
- Periods when you are completely off-line.
- Very little giving.

Let me explain the brilliance of that last piece of his counsel.

I'm a person with a high empathetic gifting. I love helping people. It fills my life with love and meaning. But due to the brokenness of my own story, my internal regulator on giving, helping, and intervening got messed up years ago. I don't know when to quit; I have a real hard time saying no. Jesus knew that to replenish my reserves, I needed to back way, way off all forms of intervening. It was a massive rescue. Because "the poor you will always have with you" (Matthew 26:11). The crises will always be there; the need will always be there.

Who gets to put a governor on your natural inclinations? I'd turn to Jesus if I were you.

The point is this—how are you going to adjust your life for recovery and resilience? You can't just slog on, burning everything you have to sustain what you think you ought to be doing. A time like ours requires real cunning. Don't let your weariness drag you right off the mountain. Make the decision to change your dailies to develop a resilient soul.

If you want resilience, you'll do it. Survivors are flexible; they adapt to the changing environment around them. Like being open to the supernatural graces and making them a normal part of life.

Let's come back to the climbing accident on Mount Hood, and why those men made such a dangerous decision. The problem with climbing (I've been a climber for many years) is that we make the summit the goal. Making it to the top is the victory. This is the objective we obsess about weeks before the event. It's the prize we have in front of us as we undertake the rigors of the ascent. The climbers on Mount Hood that fateful day made the mistake of thinking the summit was the end of their mission, and they dropped their guard. But of course they were only *halfway* to their goal. The real finish line is safely down—your car in the parking lot, or your bed at home.

For the followers of Jesus, the real finish line is either the return of Jesus or our homecoming to him.

That's why we cultivate endurance!

ALMOST THERE

———

The six men on the raft are lean and sunburned. They have been adrift in the open ocean for more than three months. Four thousand miles of the Pacific have passed under their primitive balsa log raft that could have been from 1,000 BC. Now they are approaching their greatest peril yet—a jagged barrier reef surrounding the island they hope to reach. On that reef lies the remains of a shipwreck, a grim reminder of their naked vulnerability.

The crew are making final preparations for the inevitable wreck on the reef. The last entries in the logbook read:

8:45 The wind has veered into a still more unfavorable quarter for us, so we have no hope of getting clear.

9:50 Very close now . . . all in good spirits, but it looks bad . . .

The raft smashes into the reef and is held in a death grip. Suddenly their predicament becomes violent as twenty-foot breakers pound them with brutal force:

I saw the next sea come towering up, higher than all the rest, and again I bellowed a warning aft to the others as I climbed up the stay, as high as I could get in a hurry, and hung on fast. Then I myself disappeared sideways into the midst of the green wall which towered high over us. The others, who were farther aft and saw me disappear first, estimated the height of the wall of water at twenty-five feet . . . we had all one single thought—hold on, hold on, hold, hold, hold![1]

Chapter 10

Hold On!

Remember Lot's wife!
Luke 17:32

At certain pivotal moments in our lives we face a choice, a test.

Sometimes these choices are a simple test of faith: *Will you give up sugar for Lent? Will you allow someone else to run this meeting? Will you dip into your savings to help these folks in need?* Every time we choose for God, our soul comes more into alignment with his. This is how we develop single-heartedness.

But there are moments when the test is critical: *Will you give up this relationship? Your career? This self-protection?* These crossroads are more than a trial of faith; they are a fundamental test of our *allegiance.*

The thing is, we often don't see just how critical our choice may be, especially when we're tired and distracted. These are vulnerable moments for our hearts, for in our weariness we might miss the implications of the choice.

I believe we're facing one of those moments right now. Maybe *the* moment of all moments.

Jesus saw it coming and cried out, "Remember Lot's wife!"

Why? What does she have to do with our predicament, and the ageless battle for the human heart? Well, let's go look into the story . . .

She Looked Back*

Dawn was near in the Valley of Siddim, and the wind was in the hills. A red line marked the horizon, and the valley was black. Lot ran on bleeding feet. He gripped his daughters' hands. They were wet with sweat. Lot's whole chest burned. He felt one daughter trip. "Don't stop!" he gasped. He turned and hoisted her. "Don't look back," he said. "Hurry!" he called to his wife. "The sun!"

The angels had arrived in the evening. Lot saw them first, appearing from the plain, with long shadows in front of them.

---

* This retelling of the story of Lot's wife (found in Genesis 18–19) is gratefully borrowed from an unfinished book my son Blaine Eldredge is writing, retelling many of the Old Testament stories. For more background information on this event, see Bruce Bower, "An Exploding Meteor May Have Wiped Out Ancient Dead Sea Communities," *Science News*, November 20, 2018, https://www.sciencenews.org/article/exploding-meteor-may-have-wiped-out-ancient-dead-sea-communities; Steven Collins, "Tall el-Hammam: Digging for Sodom," Tall el-Hammam Excavation Project, https://tallelhammam.com/.

Tall and lordly they seemed, with faces of judgment. There was no mistaking what they were. Lot ran to greet them, and bowed. "Please," he begged, "my lords—come into my house." There was no other safe place. The angels declined. Lot argued, beseeched, and in the end the angels agreed. So Lot led them back by secret ways through the city of Sodom.

Sodom. What a place it was. The name means "devastation." Or "to burn." Or "demons," in older Akkadian. And did it live up to those names. Together with its sister city, Gomorrah (which means "binding"), it cast a long, black shadow on the valley beyond. The streets were dangerous, and the things Lot had seen . . . well, he did not speak of them. Not that he disliked the city. He chose to live there, twice, the second time after being captured by a foreign king. There was so much to eat, and so many fine things to wear, and all the things that a wealthy city could offer.

"This is it," he said to his visitors. He pointed at a mud brick house and pushed the angels through the door. "Sit down," he urged. He kicked some dirt off the rug. "Eat!" He wrung his hands and looked for his wife. He shut the windows then, and barred the door. But someone had already seen. And the word went out—Lot had visitors, with faces like gods, and the men of the city formed a mob and came to the door. They called to Lot to hand over the angels. Lot refused. He offered his daughters. There was a fight at the door, and then one angel raised an arm and struck the whole crowd blind. He drew Lot inside.

Lot blinked until he saw the angel's face. "Lot," the angel said, "is there anyone else you need to get out? Any family?" He searched Lot's face. "We're here to destroy the town." How strange his face had looked. How stern, and sure, and *unmistakably right. How unlike a human face. Lot shook himself.* "My daughters are engaged," *he stammered,* "the men . . ."

"Get them now," *the angel commanded.*

Lot tried. He ran through the streets, past men and women with feral hungry looks, all the way to his daughters' fiancés' homes. He pounded on their doors. They appeared with sleep in their eyes and angry expressions. Lot urged and begged and cried, but the men wouldn't come. They didn't believe him. Lot left them leering in the door. His daughters hid their eyes when he told them the news.

"Go now," *the angel said.* "Go to the hills."

Lot stopped. He looked sideways at his wife. She wouldn't like that.

"Please," *Lot dared to ask,* "there's a town nearby. It's an insignificant place. No trouble at all—let us go there."

The angel consented. "Go swiftly. Do not look back. I cannot do anything until you are away. Flee."

And so Lot ran. He left the town and the things he had seen, the pride and death and vanity. He ran headlong into the desert, with his family behind him. He ran up the road, and then out to the plain, with fatigue in his eyes and his feet raising dust.

"Not much further," *he rasped, over and over again.* "We're almost there."

Until at last the sky was gray. The sun came up. Zoar was in front of them, little more than a well and a stable. Lot slowed and limped. "Zoar," *he panted. He squeezed his daughters' hands.* "We're here." *He stepped ahead.*

And then abruptly he stopped, because with a roar like a huge shrieking eagle the first stone hit. Lot pulled his daughters down, shouting for his wife. The sky blazed. Fire put strange shadows on the ground, and contrails of smoke divided the clouds. Lot had a daughter under either arm—he reached up desperately to grab his wife. The ocean sizzled and burned, and in the heat, hard winds of salt and rock strafed the hills. "Get down!" Lot screamed. He spread himself out to shield his daughters from the punishing heat.

But in the cities of suffering the brick walls turned to dust and the pots melted to glass and the fields burned away and salt lay over it all. The fire was hot as the surface of the sun, the dirt petrified, and in a moment it was done.

Huge black clouds of smoke rose up toward the tents of Abraham. Lot lifted his head. He turned, and suddenly his face was still. There was his wife, with her hands outstretched.

But not to him. To Sodom.

Lot stood.

His wife was hard and still and white as bone. Lot touched her arm. It crumbled away. Salt. Because she had looked back. But the word in Hebrew is so much more than that. She "gave her attention" to the place. She "regarded" the place. She "depended" on the place. And so she became a netsib, a "pillar," but literally, a "prefect," a "garrison," an officer of the dead watching over the dead.

Good heavens. Of all sobering stories, this is the one Jesus points to as he wraps up his warnings about our trials of the end of the age?!

Lord help us.

Whatever else the event was about, it is a tragic tale of divided allegiance and the power of this world to trap the human heart.

The Fear of Loss

Why did Lot's wife look back? She was warned by angels not to. Their stern, holy faces made it clear. Yet she looked back, *turned back* in her heart. Jesus said it had to do with her grasp for life to be good again: "Remember Lot's wife! Whoever tries to keep their life will lose it, and whoever loses their life will preserve it" (Luke 17:32–33).

She thought she would lose her life, everything she thought she needed for life, and she turned back. This is far closer to us than we might think. You see, friends, all change initially feels like loss. When you leave one life to pursue another—a career change, a shot at grad school, even something as hope-filled as a new marriage—all you know is the life you are leaving behind. The adventure ahead is still strange and unknown, and thus you are more aware of what's behind than what's ahead. So it initially feels like loss.

This doubt, this fear has crept into many good hearts in this hour.

Besides, Sodom was a thriving place, the city to be in. It was the capital of the region for about *fifteen hundred years*, beginning in 3000 BC, a symbol of might, security, and prosperity. Sodom had a wall seventeen feet thick and fifty feet high; it had palaces and temples; it had commerce and the arts. Sodom was the "well watered" plain of the Jordan that Lot saw in Genesis 13:10. Like the Nile, the Jordan would annually flood and irrigate the entire region, making Sodom lush, verdant, thriving with agriculture, food surpluses, and people.

It was also a dark and seductive place. As the capital of the region, it was the center of old-school Canaanite paganism.

The Hammam Megalithic Field—which contained fifteen hundred standing stones that rivaled Stonehenge in size—surrounded the city and was used for all kinds of dark, ritualistic activity. As my son said, "That's a really, really big number of really, really shady things."

Good Lord, people, we see in the scriptural account that the culture of the place included the routine gang-rape of newcomers. How does someone get used to such evil, acclimate to it, grow numb to its presence to overlook it for all the wonderful things the city otherwise offers?

You know the answer. You've been doing it all your life with this world we now inhabit. I mean, folks, take a look around. We turn our gaze away for understandable reasons, but this is a very evil age.

Remember Lot's wife.

This has to be one of the most cryptic, sobering, and, honestly, *unnerving* things Jesus ever said. Ever.

To be fair, I think Lot's wife had a sort of trauma bond with the city of Sodom. A trauma bond is a tragic tie that forms between an abuser and their victim. It happens when evil gets its hooks in you from living too close to it. In spite of those ties, in spite of every pull this world gains over us, Jesus is urging us, *Do not look back. No divided hearts; no divided allegiances.*

Everything for Your Everything

I said in chapter 3 that the pandemic was an apocalypse—which means a "revealing," or exposing. Among all that has been revealed, the most concerning is our divided allegiances.

The fear that overcame all of us in varying degrees revealed that our security was not as firmly established in Christ as we thought. The grasping for life to be good again revealed that our hope was not exactly centered in Christ either. Now the Falling Away is revealing how deep our disappointments with God actually run, how easily these shallow roots can be upended.

Through the preceding chapters I've described a number of the effects of the global trauma on me—my compulsive buying, the fixing up of our home, the little comforts I've turned to. I'm also having the most interesting experience: memories keep coming up of goodness long past. I'm remembering moments from trips taken years ago and experiencing sweet nostalgia from my childhood. I'm not one to reminisce much, but it's happening a good deal, almost unbidden—thinking of great times gone by and wondering how to get them back again.

Was this happening to Lot's wife as she ran across the plain?

Throughout God's long, tempestuous love affair with the human race recorded in both Testaments, the central dilemma has always been, and will always be, double-mindedness. The lack of wholeheartedness. "These people honor me with their lips, but their hearts are far from me" (Matthew 15:8).

The real danger is when you seem to have secured your life again. You finally quit your job, you moved to a new place, you fell in love. Because of everything we've covered here—the trauma, the fear of deprivation, the utter relief of having life good again—your heart quietly says, *I'm good, I don't need anything now.* The thought of the return of Christ disappears like an early morning fog burned away by noon. Let some other generation deal with that.

> Your love is like the morning mist,
> like the early dew that disappears. (Hosea 6:4)

The snare the enemy set for our hearts was to afflict us, traumatize us, tempt us, and get our hearts to land in a place where we sigh, feel relief, and say, *I'm good. This is good.* Without God. A taste of the kingdom without the King.

During the spring and summer of 2020, Stasi found herself enjoying a new distraction. She spent hours and hours on her laptop, looking at cottages for sale in Ireland and Scotland. It was a lovely detachment from the crisis, and dreaming is actually good for the soul. Besides, we have a long history with those countries. They are part of our lineage, we have dear friends who live there, and we feel a missional pull to minister there. But what our *hearts* remember is idyllic moments we've shared there on vacation, the kind of holiday where everything is right and wonderful, and the world felt a million miles away.

Stasi's obsession began in the quarantines, but it has carried on. Because the longing for life to be good again is not subsiding; it is growing stronger in every human heart.

Just this morning she told me, "I found an estate for sale on the west coast of the Scottish Highlands. Near that little village we love. It has its own loch and streams!" I was kind of surprised this came up again, after all the soul-work we've done. We've walked through the practices in this book together, tending our recovery and resilience. *An estate in the highlands? My wife has lost her mind.* I was already dismissing it when she added, "There's red stag hunting and fly-fishing on the property!"

Suddenly I see it—the heathered hills sweeping up to craggy peaks. The cascading streams bubbling down through mossy meadows. The loch with a little boat drawn up on the pebbled beach. Sunlight sparkling on the ocean as the sun sinks into the west. A fire in the fireplace and a dram of single malt on the table in our little white house overlooking it all.

Quicker than any mental reflection, my heart did a one-eighty. *Done.* I was ready to cash in our retirement and buy the place, sell everything we have, leave our loved ones and work behind to go get our little slice of happiness and respite. *Let the world collapse, I don't care. I'm done with all this. When can we move?*

I'm standing in the kitchen on a fairly ordinary Saturday afternoon watching the ancient battle for the human heart play out in my soul. Because I'm stressed out and traumatized and I just want a break. I want life to be good.

Remember Lot's wife.

I shudder at how easily my heart can be divided. I do love God, I really do. I know you do too. The double-mindedness is revealed when we only *sort of* want God. Our longing for life to be good again becomes the test we hold up against God—if he seems to be helping, wonderful. We believe. If he doesn't, well . . . we're going to chase whatever we think will fill our longing and get back to God sometime down the road. Powerful, ancient forces are pulling us in that direction.

We are in such a vulnerable moment.

We must, we must, we must choose single-heartedness, where we desire Jesus above everything else—above all our other "lovers," our false Edens, our passing comforts.

If you want to become a wholehearted person, you must reach the point where happily, lovingly, you give absolutely everything over to God. You make Jesus your everything, your all-in-all. Not only is this the fulfillment of your heart's created destiny, it is the source of all recovery and resilience. Nothing can be taken from you because you've already surrendered everything.

Those flowers on the porch that I've been nursing? I noticed this morning that dry rot is creeping over my favorite hanging basket. And in another pot some pest is munching holes through every bloom. You can't hold on to things, friends; there's no looking back. It doesn't do any good, but it *can* do an enormous amount of harm. Remember Lot's wife.

You can't go back, especially at a time when God is moving things forward. He wants us to come along with him.

I give everything for your everything.

This is now my prayer.

I give everything for your everything.

A few friends of mine have very deep and special relationships with God. They hear from him, receive visions of the things he is doing on the earth. Recently one of them sent me an account of a vision he had of the actual scene-behind-the-scenes in this great hour. He did not know I

If you want to become a wholehearted person, you must reach the point where happily, lovingly, you give absolutely everything over to God. You make Jesus your everything, your all-in-all.

was writing this book; he had not heard a word about this chapter. Yet this is what he sent:

> During the battle at the end, many people lost their faith, like Lot's wife (Genesis 19:26). They walked away from holiness, turned, not seen clearly, and had essentially sided with the enemy. Right at the end. Sadly, very sadly, some just didn't make it—many of whom had been expected to right up to the end.

The Secret to the Longing

But we are not like those who turn away from God to their own destruction. We are the faithful ones, whose souls will be saved. (Hebrews 10:39 NLT)

I wonder—could our heightened state of longing for things to be good again be far more than a response to trauma, chronic disappointment, and deprivation? Might it actually be pointing to something wonderful?

If the heavens are thrilling as they stage for the return of Christ, if the battle on earth is raging, if Christ himself is standing at the door—wouldn't our hearts somehow recognize it? He who is our heart of hearts, our deepest desire, and most sincere longing, is drawing near—nearer than ever before. This would be especially moving for those in whom Christ dwells. Maybe—just maybe—our hearts are responding to the imminent return of Jesus while our rational minds continue to dismiss the thought.

When the moon comes closest to the earth in its orbital swing—what is called the perigee of the moon—the gravitational pull on the earth is strongest. A few times each year, the perigee coincides with a full moon and the gravitational attraction is strong indeed, causing tidal upheaval and flooding. Many scientists believe that the moon was once a part of the earth, that it broke away during a catastrophic event and now orbits like an estranged lover. When it draws near, the earth feels its presence deeply.[2]

Wouldn't our hearts do the same?

This is the greatest love story ever told, the Sacred Romance. As the Hero approaches from his long sojourn, his bride knows in her heart that he's coming—like the lovers in the song who can feel each other's heartbeat "for a thousand miles."[3]

Compasses are known to behave strangely as they near magnetic north. A compass induced to start spinning while close to what has pulled it all these years will continue spinning until something slows and stops it.[4] Perhaps all this crazy and erratic human behavior in this hour might indicate the loss of bearing that comes when something strong begins to overwhelm our *internal* compasses. Someone is approaching.

What sort of magnetic pull would the approach of our Lord and Master have on the hearts that love him?

Stasi and I have two golden retrievers. I sometimes call them "lampreys," because they cling to us whenever we're around. If we get up and move to another room, they will always get up and follow, every time, then lie happily again at our feet (as they are doing right now while I write this). Whenever we leave the house, they are desolate, and

What sort of magnetic pull
would the approach of our
Lord and Master have on
the hearts that love him?

whenever Stasi or I draw near to home, as we are pulling into the neighborhood but several houses away, our goldens will wake up, even from a deep nap, run to the garage door, and stand there wagging their happy tails. They know when their masters are approaching.

I wonder if our hearts are doing the same thing. There is an ache, awakening down in the depths of our hearts that nothing else can assuage.

Soon, Friends

When I was a boy I read every adventure and survival story I could get my hands on.

One book that particularly captured my imagination was Thor Heyerdal's *Kon-Tiki*, his personal account of a wild and dangerous trip he and five other Norse men took across the open Pacific—from the coast of Peru to Polynesia—to prove a theory that Polynesia was first settled from the west and not the east. These guys spent three months in utter isolation, adrift, using the wind and ocean currents to guide their craft—a primitive balsa wood raft, modeled after those used by the coastal Indians before the time of Christ. This was their home, their sanctuary and lifeboat for 101 days and 4,300 miles.

Thor and his crew crossed sections of the Pacific no one ever sees, living on fish they caught, accompanied by dolphins, whales—and sharks, constantly. They braved violent storms. They lolled around the deck on sunny days while the raft was carried on by the silent, powerful currents.

As a boy I loved the wild freedom of this true tale, the raw experience of nature. Plus, I was a confirmed fisherman from my youth, and the thought of fishing every day, any day when the fancy caught you over a three-month idyll sounded like heaven to me.

For some reason I picked up the book again this summer. I was drawn to it. There was something about the story of a great ordeal I needed for these days. Stories help to orient us. They give us perspective and strength. This time around, what absolutely grabbed my heart was the account of their arrival in Polynesia. After 101 days at sea, with paradise finally in sight, their log raft was smashed into the jaws of the reef surrounding an uninhabited island. Salvation lay only a hundred yards beyond the lagoon, but the men were trapped under massive waves by the grip of the reef:

A new sea rose high up astern of us like a glittering, green glass wall. As we sank down it came rolling after us, and, in the same second in which I saw it high above me, I felt a violent blow and was submerged under floods of water. I felt the suction through my whole body, with such great power that I had to strain every single muscle in my frame and think of one thing only—hold on, hold on!

The whole submersion lasted only seconds, but it demanded more endurance than we usually have in our bodies. There is greater strength in the human mechanism than that of the muscles alone. I determined that, if I was to die, I would die in this position, like a knot on the stay. The sea thundered on, over and past, and as it roared by it revealed a hideous sight. . . . The vessel we knew from weeks and months at sea was no more; in a few seconds our pleasant world had become a shattered wreck.[5]

Something deep in my soul resonated with the pounding—the need to hold, hold, hold on while the world we knew shattered around us.

Then, as I read on, the real gift came—the men made it safely to the island:

I shall never forget that wade across the reef toward the heavenly palm island that grew larger as it came to meet us. When I reached the sunny sand beach, I slipped off my shoes and thrust my bare toes down into the warm, bone-dry sand. It was as though I enjoyed the sight of every footprint which dug itself into the virgin sand beach that led up to the palm trunks. Soon the palm tops closed over my head, and I went on, right in toward the center of the tiny island. Green coconuts hung under the palm tufts, and some luxuriant bushes were thickly covered with snow-white blossoms, which smelled so sweet and seductive that I felt quite faint. In the interior of the island two quite tame terns flew about my shoulders. They were as white and light as wisps of cloud.

I was completely overwhelmed. I sank down on my knees and thrust my fingers deep down into the dry warm sand.

The voyage was over. We were all alive. We had run ashore on a small uninhabited South Sea island. And what an island! Torstein came in, flung away a sack, threw himself flat on his back and looked up at the palm tops and the white birds, light as down, which circled noiselessly just above us. Soon we were all six lying there. Herman, always energetic, climbed up a small palm and pulled down a cluster of large green coconuts. We cut off their soft tops with our machete knives, as if they were eggs, and poured down our throats the most delicious refreshing drink in the world—sweet, cold milk from young and seedless palm fruit. On the reef outside resounded the monotonous drum beats from the guard at the gates of paradise.

"Purgatory was a bit damp," said Bengt, "but heaven is more or less as I'd imagined it."

We stretched ourselves luxuriously on the ground and smiled up at the white trade-wind clouds drifting by westward up above the palm tops. Now we were no longer following them helplessly; now we lay on a fixed, motionless island, in Polynesia.

And as we lay and stretched ourselves, the breakers outside us rumbled like a train, to and fro, to and fro, all along the horizon.

Bengt was right; this was heaven.[6]

I let out a long, deep sigh. This is such a beautiful, reassuring picture of our odyssey to the new earth, our homecoming, wandering in Eden and simply letting it heal us for a while. We are all of us, always, looking for some version of this. Beneath the surface of our busy and besieged lives, our Eden hearts are always searching for home.

And isn't it striking that the most dangerous part of

their journey came right at the end of the survival story? Just like ours. The men made it through because they didn't let go. They acted like survivors till the end; they held on.

We are so close, friends. Guaranteed. There's no need to fear or grasp or look back.

So what shall we do?

We take the things in this book seriously. We rearrange our lives to center around God, so that we might take hold of the strength that prevails. We handle our recovery and resilience as seriously as any survivor would. Return to chapter 9 and finish your prescription with Jesus.† Then hold on to it! Is there someone you've been thinking about as you have read this book? Make sure they have a copy too!

We remember Lot's wife, as our Lord commanded. Every time our hearts are tempted to look back, we redouble our love for Jesus, knowing that strong, dark currents are trying to pull us away. We take hold of the supernatural graces! We give everything for his everything, diving deep in our innermost being to find the God who gives us resilience.

His resilience will not fail us. Soon we will be laughing and singing with healed hearts, as we walk with Jesus in a completely healed world.

---

† Honestly, given the endless distractions of the world, our weary soul, and "COVID brain," seriously consider rereading this entire book or, better yet, listen to the audiobook. I've added a lot of spontaneous content there, and the guided prayers at the end of each chapter are accompanied with music and are quite profound.

Prayers

River of Life

Jesus, I come back to you now in my longing for life to be good again. I love you here, Lord, in my soul's heartache. I consecrate to you my Primal Drive for Life. I surrender to you my ability to aspire for good things, plan for them, take hold of them, enjoy them, and keep on aspiring. I consecrate all living in me to you, Lord Jesus; I give you my famished craving for life to be good again. I love you here. I love you right here. And now I ask that the river of your life would flow in me, in my Primal Drive for Life and in my longing for life to be good again. I open my heart and soul to the river of life. Let it flow in me, through me, and all around me—restoring, renewing, and healing me. You alone are the life I seek, and I welcome your river into my heart and soul; I receive the river of your life in me. Thank you, God! In your mighty name I pray.

Strength That Prevails

Father, Jesus, Holy Spirit—God of all creation, God of the thunderstorm and the waterfall, I need your strength. I need the strength that prevails. I don't want to fall away; I don't want to lose heart. I choose you above all things. I give you my allegiance and my undivided love. I choose single-heartedness toward you, Lord Jesus—body, soul, and spirit; heart, mind, and will. I pray for a supernatural resilience, God. Fill me with your overcoming strength, a victorious strength. Father, Lord of heaven and earth, strengthen me. I pray for strength of mind, strength of heart, strength of will. I pray for the strength that allows me to escape all that is coming against the saints in this hour. Fill me with resilience. By faith I receive it and thank you for it. In Jesus' name, amen.

Glory

Father, Jesus, Holy Spirit, I receive your Glory into my being. I receive the Glory that fills the oceans, the Glory that sustains the sun. I receive the Glory that raised Christ from the dead! I pray that your Eden Glory would fill my heart, soul, mind, and strength. I am your temple, Lord; come and fill your temple with your Glory! I also pray that your Eden Glory would shield me against all forms of Desolation coming over my life. I renounce every agreement I might have made with Desolation, every agreement large and small. I choose you, God. I renounce the Falling Away and

I choose you. Regardless of how I feel, I choose you, Lord. You are my God and Savior. I pray that your Eden Glory would fill my life—restoring me, renewing me, granting me supernatural endurance and resilience. I also invoke your Eden Glory over my life as a shield, over my household and domain. I invoke your glory, love, and kingdom as my constant strength and shield. In the name of the Lord Jesus Christ, ruler of heaven and earth. Thank you, Lord!

Abundance

Creator of my soul, Creator of all mother-love and mother-need, I need you here.

I need your mother-love. I need the assurance of abundance. I need the benediction of my being. I need a deep, bonded love with you. I need attachment here, in the place of my soul you created for attachment. Come, healing God, and heal me here in the place of mother. I open my story of mothering to you, God. I invite you into my need for primal love, primal nourishment. Nourish me here, just as you promised.

Creator of my soul, Creator of all mother-love and mother-need, I invite you into my need for primal connection. I invite you into my need for the primal blessing of my being, my existence.

Forgive me for taking this need to other places. I am giving all this to you, God; I am opening it to you now. I forgive my mom. I do. I forgive her and release her, and I invite your mother-love and mother nourishment, your comfort and solace into this place in my soul. Fill me with attachment love; fill me with the assurance of abundance. Come into my primal fears that there will not be enough for me, and fill me with the assurance of abundance. In Jesus' name, amen.

Christ in You

I renounce all hatred. I renounce every agreement I've been making with hatred in any form. I renounce all cooperation or participation with hatred. I also renounce all hatred coming against me; I reject it from my life. My Father loves me. The Lord Jesus loves me. I choose the way of love. I choose love! So now I proclaim and enforce the mighty love of God against all hatred coming against me, in the name of Jesus Christ. I pray the shield of your love, Father, to protect my heart and soul from every attack of hatred. In Jesus' name, amen.

Acknowledgments

M y profound thanks to Luke Eldredge, who provided invaluable research for this project, and to the teams at Yates & Yates and Thomas Nelson who have helped bring this critical message into your hands.

Notes

Introduction: No Ordinary Moment

1. Paulo Coelho, *The Alchemist*, trans. Alan R. Clarke (New York: HarperOne, 1993), 116.

2. Ed Yong, "What Happens When Americans Can Finally Exhale: The Pandemic's Mental Wounds Are Still Wide Open," *Atlantic*, May 20, 2021, https://www.theatlantic.com/health/archive/2021/05/pandemic-trauma-summer/618934/.

Chapter 1: I Just Want Life to Be Good Again

1. Wilfred Thesiger, "From *Arabian Sands*," in *Points Unknown: The Greatest Adventure Writing of the Twentieth Century*, ed. David Roberts (New York: W. W. Norton, 2000), 93, 95.

2. George Eliot, *The Mill on the Floss* (1880; repr., New York: Penguin Classics, 2003), 314.

3. Daniel Ladinsky, ed., *Love Poems from God* (New York: Penguin, 2002), 300.

4. So much home improvement occurred nationwide that the shortage of building supplies drove lumber prices up 300 percent or more, adding $36,000 to the cost of a new home. Porch Research, "Survey: Home Improvement Trends in the Time of Covid," Porch, July 21, 2020, https://porch.com/advice/home-improvement-trends-covid; Frank Morris, "Why Home Improvement Has Surged and How It's Changing America," NPR, September 11, 2020, https://www.npr.org/2020/09/11/909264580/why-home-improvement-has-surged-and-how-its-changing-america;

"Framing Lumber Prices," National Association of Homebuilders, last updated November 12, 2021, https://www.nahb.org/news-and-economics/housing-economics/national-statistics/framing-lumber-prices.

5. Dan B. Allender and Cathy Loerzel, *Redeeming Heartache: How Past Suffering Reveals Our True Calling* (Grand Rapids, MI: Zondervan, 2021).

6. Dana Rose Garfin, E. Alison Holman, and Roxane Cohen Silver, "Cumulative Exposure to Prior Collective Trauma and Acute Stress Responses to the Boston Marathon Bombings," *Psychological Science* 26, no. 6 (2015): 675–83, doi.org/10.1177/0956797614561043.

7. For the full story, see Edward Dolnick, *Down the Great Unknown: John Wesley Powell's 1869 Journey of Discovery and Tragedy Through the Grand Canyon* (New York: HarperCollins, 2001).

8. "How Many Israelites Left Egypt in the Exodus?," Got Questions, accessed November 19, 2021, https://www.gotquestions.org/Israelites-exodus.html.

9. Richard Gunderman, "For the Young Doctor About to Burn Out," *Atlantic*, February 21, 2014, http://www.theatlantic.com/health/archive/2014/02/for-the-young-doctor-about-to-burn-out/284005/.

Chapter 2: Where Are We? What's Happening?

1. John Muir, "A Perilous Night on Mount Shasta," *The Wild Muir: Twenty-Two of John Muir's Greatest Adventures*, ed. Lee Stetson (El Portal, CA: Yosemite Conservancy, 1994), 122–23.

2. Rudyard Kipling, "If—," *Kipling: Poems*, selected by Peter Washington (London: Alfred A. Knopf, 2007), 170.

3. Hongmi Lee, Buddhika Bellana, and Janice Chen, "What Can Narratives Tell Us About the Neural Bases of Human Memory?," *Current Opinion in Behavioral Sciences* 32 (April 2020): 111–19, https://doi.org/10.1016/j.cobeha.2020.02.007.

4. Joshua J. Mark, "Roman Empire," *World History Encyclopedia*, March 22, 2018, https://www.worldhistory.org/Roman_Empire/.

5. Spencer Mizen, "Genghis Khan: The Mongol Warlord Who Almost Conquered the World," History Extra, accessed November 19, 2021, https://www.historyextra.com/period/medieval/genghis-khan-mongol-warlord-conquered-world-china-medieval/.

6. John C. McManus, *Fire and Fortitude: The US Army in the Pacific War, 1941–1943* (New York: Penguin, 2019), 22.

7. Douglas Cobb, *And Then the End Will Come: The Completion of the Great Commission and Nine Other Clues That Jesus Is Coming Soon* (Louisville, KY: DeepWater Books, 2021), 44–45.

Chapter 3: The Strength That Prevails

1. John Muir, "A Perilous Night on Mount Shasta," *The Wild Muir: Twenty-Two of John Muir's Greatest Adventures,* ed. Lee Stetson (El Portal, CA: Yosemite Conservancy, 1994), 125, 127.

2. "He offered up prayers and petitions with fervent cries and tears" (Hebrews 5:7).

3. *Strong's Concordance,* s.v. "2729. katischuó," Bible Hub, accessed November 20, 2021, https://biblehub.com/greek/2729.htm.

4. William Shakespeare, *Henry V,* act 4, scene 1.

5. Charles Bellinger, "Summary of Kierkegaard's *The Sickness unto Death,*" Texas Christian University, March 2005, https://lib.tcu .edu/staff/bellinger/60023/summary_of_sicknessUD.htm.

Chapter 4: Eden Glory, Not Desolation

1. John Eldredge, *Get Your Life Back: Everyday Practices for a World Gone Mad* (Nashville: Thomas Nelson, 2020).

2. Jennifer K. Logue et al., "Sequelae in Adults at 6 Months After COVID-19 Infection," *JAMA Network Open* 4, no 2 (February 19, 2021), https://jamanetwork.com/journals /jamanetworkopen/fullarticle/2776560.

3. Ed Yong, "What Happens When Americans Can Finally Exhale: The Pandemic's Mental Wounds Are Still Wide Open," *Atlantic,* May 20, 2021, https://www.theatlantic.com/health/archive /2021/05/pandemic-trauma-summer/618934/.

Chapter 5: The Assurance of Abundance

1. Laura Hillenbrand, *Unbroken: A World War II Story of Survival, Resilience, and Redemption* (New York: Random House, 2010), 132.

2. Robert Karen, *Becoming Attached: First Relationships and How They Shape Our Capacity to Love* (New York: Oxford University Press, 1998), 382.

3. Penny Simkin et al., *Pregnancy, Childbirth and the Newborn*, 4th ed. (Minnetonka, MN: Meadowbrook Press, 2010), 398.

4. There is so much literature on this point it is impossible to pick a representative sample, but this article is a beginning: Karleen D. Gribble, "Mental Health, Attachment, and Breastfeeding: Implications for Adopted Children and Their Mothers," *International Breastfeeding Journal* 1, no. 5 (2006), https://doi.org/10.1186/1746-4358-1-5.

5. Laurence Gonzales, *Deep Survival: Who Lives, Who Dies, and Why* (New York: W. W. Norton, 2005), 156.

6. "How Long Do Babies Carry Their Mother's Immunity?," National Health Services, last updated June 9, 2021, https://www.nhs.uk/common-health-questions/childrens-health/how-long-do-babies-carry-their-mothers-immunity.

7. Dallas Willard, *The Divine Conspiracy: Rediscovering Our Hidden Life in God* (New York: HarperCollins, 2014), 117.

8. Gary W. Moon, ed., *Eternal Living* (Downers Grove, IL: InterVarsity Press, 2015), 16.

9. Karen, *Becoming Attached*, 23.

10. Karen, 15.

11. Karen, 55.

12. Jim Wilder, *Renovated: God, Dallas Willard, and the Church That Transforms* (Colorado Springs: NavPress, 2020), 1, 6.

13. Karen, *Becoming Attached*, 7.

14. Wilder, *Renovated*, 6.

15. To explore this more deeply, see Rankin Wilbourne, *Union with Christ* (Colorado Springs: David C. Cook, 2016), and chapter 13 of my book *Get Your Life Back*.

16. Henry Scougal, *The Life of God in the Soul of Man* (1677; repr., Louisville, KY: GLH Publishing, 2015), 5.

17. Wilder, *Renovated*, 6.

Chapter 6: Unconverted Places

1. Jon Krakauer, *Into Thin Air: A Personal Account of the Mt. Everest Disaster* (New York: Random House, 1997), chapter 18.

2. Walter Hooper, "Preface," *God in the Dock: Essays on Theology and Ethics* (1970; repr., Cambridge: William B. Eerdmans, 2014), xiv.

3. Theodore Roosevelt, *Hunting Trips of a Ranchman and the*

Wilderness Hunter (1885; repr., New York: The Modern Library, 1996), 436–37.

4. George MacDonald, *Unspoken Sermons Series I, II, and III* (1867; repr., New York: Start Publishing, 2012), 167.

Chapter 7: The Kingdom Without the King

1. Steven Rinella, *Meat Eater: Adventures from the Life of an American Hunter* (New York: Spiegel & Grau, 2012), 9–10.
2. *The Edge of Paradise*, produced by John Wehrheim, directed by Robert C. Stone (Wehrheim Productions, 2009), https://theedgeofparadisefilm.com/about/.
3. Pankaj Mishra, "What Are the Cultural Revolution's Lessons for Our Current Moment?," *New Yorker*, January 25, 2021, https://www.newyorker.com/magazine/2021/02/01/what-are-the-cultural-revolutions-lessons-for-our-current-moment.
4. Derek Thompson, "The Great Resignation Is Accelerating," *Atlantic*, October 15, 2021, https://www.theatlantic.com/ideas/archive/2021/10/great-resignation-accelerating/620382/; Phil Reed, "Millions of Americans Quitting Their Jobs During 'The Great Resignation,'" MSN, June 24, 2021, https://www.msn.com/en-us/money/careersandeducation/millions-of-americans-quitting-their-jobs-during-the-great-resignation/ar-AALpHn9.
5. John Eldredge, *All Things New: Heaven, Earth, and the Restoration of Everything You Love* (Nashville: Thomas Nelson, 2017), 12, 14–16.

Chapter 8: The Deep Well Inside Us

1. Russ McCarrell and Zachary Behr, directors, *Alone*, season 8, episode 10, "All In," aired August 12, 2021, on HISTORY, streaming video, 1:02:13, https://www.history.com/shows/alone/season-8/episode-10.
2. Nicholas Carr, *The Shallows: What the Internet Is Doing to Our Brains* (New York: W. W. Norton, 2010).
3. Jeanne Guyon, *Union with God* (Sargent, GA: Seedsowers, 1981), 1.
4. "Here I am! I stand at the door and knock. If anyone hears my voice and opens the door, I will come in" (Revelation 3:20).
5. Catholic News Service, "Pope's Message: Prayer Is a Constant Learning Experience," *St. Louis Review*, December 7, 2018, https://www.archstl.org/popes-message-prayer-is-a-constant-learning-experience-3406.

6. Theophan the Recluse in *The Art of Prayer: An Orthodox Anthology*, comp. Igumen Chariton of Valamo, trans. E. Kadloubovsky and E. M. Palmer, ed. Timothy Ware (London: Faber and Faber, 1966), 110.

7. John Eldredge, *Get Your Life Back: Everyday Practices for a World Gone Mad* (Nashville: Thomas Nelson, 2020), 16.

8. Eldredge, *Get Your Life Back*, 24, 25.

Chapter 9: Your Prescription

1. Laurence Gonzales, *Deep Survival: Who Lives, Who Dies, and Why* (New York: W. W. Norton, 2017), 120.

2. C. S. Lewis, *Mere Christianity* (1952; repr., New York: HarperOne, 1980), 50.

3. "Sports Injuries," MedBroadcast, accessed November 20, 2021, https://medbroadcast.com/condition/getcondition/sports-injuries.

4. Jayne Leonard, "How to Build Muscle with Exercise," Medical News Today, January 8, 2020, https://www.medicalnewstoday .com/articles/319151.

5. Jeffrey Zimmerman and Marie-Nathalie Beaudoin, "Neurobiology for Your Narrative: How Brain Science Can Influence Narrative Work," *Journal of Systemic Therapies* 34 no. 2 (August 2015): 59–74, https://doi.org/10.1521/jsyt.2015.34.2.59.

6. Sebastian Junger, *War* (New York: Hachette, 2010), 23.

7. Alan Jacobs, *The Narnian: The Life and Imagination of C. S. Lewis* (New York: HarperOne, 2008), 299.

8. Gonzales, *Deep Survival*, 40.

9. Bakari Akil II, "How the Navy Seals Increased Passing Rates: Better Passing Rates Through Simple Psychology," *Psychology Today*, November 9, 2009, https://www.psychologytoday.com /us/blog/communication-central/200911/how-the-navy-seals -increased-passing-rates.

10. Roald Amundsen, *My Life as an Explorer* (New York: Doubleday, 1927).

11. Gonzales, *Deep Survival*, 105.

12. Mark Matousek, "The Meeting Eyes of Love: How Empathy Is Born in Us," *Psychology Today*, April 8, 2011, https://www .psychologytoday.com/us/blog/ethical-wisdom/201104/the -meeting-eyes-love-how-empathy-is-born-in-us.

13. Mark 16:6; John 14:1; Luke 21:34 AMP.

14. *Strong's Concordance*, s.v. "916. bareó," Bible Hub, accessed November 21, 2021, https://biblehub.com/greek/916.htm.

Chapter 10: Hold On!

1. Thor Heyerdal, *Kon-Tiki* (1950; repr., New York: Skyhorse Publishing, 2014), 65, 189, 192.
2. NOAA, "What Is a Perigean Spring Tide?," National Oceanic and Atmospheric Administration, last updated February 26, 2021, https://oceanservice.noaa.gov/facts/perigean-spring-tide.html; "Moon Facts," *National Geographic*, July 16, 2004, https://www .nationalgeographic.com/science/article/moon-facts.
3. Van Morrison, vocalist, "Crazy Love," by Van Morrison, recorded 1969, track 3 on *Moondance*, Warner Brothers, 33 1/3 rpm, 2:34.
4. "What Happens When a Compass Is Taken to the Site of Magnetic Pole of Earth?," Physics Stack Exchange, August 13, 2015, https:// physics.stackexchange.com/questions/200152/what-happens -when-a-compass-is-taken-to-the-site-of-magnetic-pole-of-earth.
5. Heyerdal, *Kon-Tiki*, 191–93.
6. Heyerdal, 197–98.

About the Author

John Eldredge is a bestselling author and counselor. He is also president of Wild at Heart, a ministry devoted to helping people discover the heart of God and recover their own hearts in God's love. John and his wife, Stasi, live near Colorado Springs, Colorado. To learn more, visit wildatheart.org.

Experience
"30 Days to Resilience"
in the **Pause App**.

*"I've developed a simple plan to help you become resilient.
It's the beginning of a new way of living.
Your soul is going to thank you."*

PauseApp.com

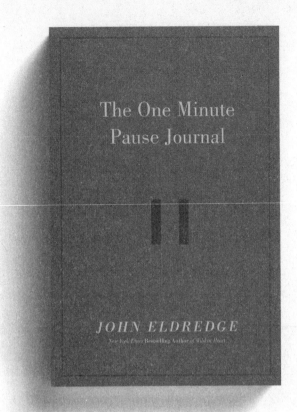

The One Minute Pause Journal

This 90-day guided journal is a simple daily practice that will deepen your connection with God through small moments of reflection and relaxation.

Each entry features...

- A set of morning and evening prompts
- Scripture
- Prayers
- Journaling space for you to engage your soul and find deeper union with God

Available now at your favorite bookstore.

get your life back

A refreshing guide to recover your life through simple practices including...

- The One Minute Pause
- Benevolent detachment
- Getting outside
- Stepping back from technology

Book and companion video series and study guide available now at your favorite bookstore.

JOHN ELDREDGE

WILD AT HEART

PODCAST

Wild at Heart offers weekly podcast conversations with John Eldredge and his team. It's free. It's powerful. And it's better when you're in the conversation with us.

Listen on
Apple Podcasts

Listen on
Spotify Podcasts

Listen on
Google Podcasts